Scott Reeves is a freelance writer and publisher
who has been a keen stock car fan
since his first trip to Odsal Stadium in 1987.
This is his first book.

GOLD TOP

The John Lund Story

Scott Reeves

Chequered Flag PUBLISHING

Published in the UK by Chequered Flag Publishing
PO Box 4669, Sheffield, S6 9ET
www.chequeredflagpublishing.co.uk

A CIP record for this book is available from the British Library

ISBN 978-0-9569460-0-3

Printed in the UK by Henry Ling Limited

Picture Acknowledgements
Mike Greenwood, Photostox: pp vi, 56, 102, 120, 140, 160, 176,
190, 208, 222, 238, 252, 274, 287
Norman & Brenda Lund: pp 4, 20, 38, 82
Scott Reeves: pp iv, 270

Dedicated to the memory of Sam Lund
1988-2007

A proportion of the price of this book
will be donated to the
British Stock Car Drivers Association
Benevolent Fund

Contents

Acknowledgements

This book would have been impossible to produce without the help and blessing of its star: John Lund. I tentatively approached him in the pits at Birmingham Wheels Raceway, not sure whether he would want to be put under the spotlight since he had shied away from the cameras during a recent BBC documentary. On the particular evening I spoke to him, John had just arrived and was striding towards the his car in his distinctive orange racing suit.

'I'm supposed to be on track in a couple of minutes, and I've not signed in yet. Come back after the first heat.'

Despite running late - a usual occurance, I soon learned - John made time to speak to me between races. A glimmer of a smile flashed across his face as I described what I wanted to write.

'Why not Willie Harrison?' John asked a few days later. 'Surely nobody wants to read about me?'

So modesty was another Lund trait alongside unpunctuality.

Months passed, and the book slowly took shape. John cheerfully put up with all the interviews, phone calls, fact-checking and photograph requests. Thanks John, this book wouldn't have seen the light of day without your help.

Thanks are also due to Annette, Norman and Brenda Lund, each of whom gave up their time to be interviewed. The 'other' John Lund, Ian Higgins and Andy Hodgson also helped clear up specific questions and issues.

The stock car community is blessed with a number of periodicals and magazines that helped with research, but a special mention must be made of www.briscaf1stox.co.uk, a vast online archive of stock car results and a treasure trove for historians of this particular motorsport.

Paul Hines is one of stock car racing's best ambassadors and he has provided an excellent foreword. I hope he can match John's achievements over an equally long and successful career.

Mike Greenwood graciously adhered to my tight deadlines and provided some excellent images that decorate the text. Much-needed advice was generously offered by Patricia Eve of Seafarer Books and Neil Randon. Various drafts of the manuscript were read by Ivan Cartwright-Terry, Chris Parry, Gary Reeves and Lee Reeves. Thank you all for your comments, although any mistakes must remain my own.

Finally, the biggest thanks of all must go to my wife Roisin. Perhaps she made a mistake by suggesting I write a book on stock cars, because she consigned herself to months of isolation as I sat in the study poring over this book instead of being with her.

Or maybe that was her plan all along?

Foreword

By Paul Hines

One of my proudest moments as a stock car driver was when I finally got to superstar and I lined up next to John Lund. It was a weird feeling. I've been a fan since I was four or five years old, and John has been around all that time. I felt like I'd made it as a stock car driver because of who I was with on the grid.

That first meeting as a superstar was at Coventry. I was a bit nervous and excited as I sat in the car ready to go in the meeting final. The yellow flags came out to send us on the rolling lap and at that point I looked across at John. He hadn't even got his gloves on! I was stressed out for him, thinking 'bloody hell John, come on, we're about to go and you've not even got your neck brace or your gloves on yet!' He slowly put one glove on. The blue grade drivers were off by this point, the reds were just about to go. I'm all geared up, ready to go, looking across at John, who painfully slowly put his other glove on, one finger at a time. I could not believe how calm he was. I wanted to get out of the car and dress him myself!

But that's the sort of guy that John is. Nothing stresses him, and it certainly shows in his racing. He is such a nice guy to talk to off the track, but on the track he has an unshakeable coolness. I can tell he is never worried about another driver being near him on track. I've never seen John put a foot wrong because someone else is behind him, even when they have been faster, and there are only a few occasions when that was the case. He never seems flustered or worried; he rarely goes wide and lets a car past. I think that has been one of the main reasons for his success. He is unflappable. You can never intimidate him. He has never cracked, never made a mistake because he was nervous. When you race against him you can tell he is tremendously skilful. You've got to have massive respect for someone like that.

Perhaps sometimes we forget what a massive impact John has had on stock car racing. Car design, driving technique, the set-up of the car, the whole Formula 1 stock car landscape has been changed by John Lund. Who knows where the sport or the cars would be without his influence?

It makes you proud to be a stock car driver when you race with somebody like John. It's almost a pleasure to get hit by him. It's a pleasure to hit him too, not that I do that very often! I am sure I speak on behalf of everyone in stock car racing when I say how lucky we are to have witnessed and continue to witness John behind the wheel.

He's a legend, there's no other word to describe him.

Preface

Relief.

Not the emotion you would expect from a sportsman who was about to win his first World Championship.

Joy, maybe. Or exhilaration. Or ecstasy.

Yet as John Lund rounded the final turn of the final lap, his stock car sliding on the shale surface, he merely felt relief.

For 25 laps he had led the most important race of the year. He knew that there were no drivers close enough to challenge him. In truth, it was one of the most one-sided World Finals that anybody could remember.

But John spent the whole race waiting for something to go wrong. Maybe the car would develop a mechanical fault. Maybe one of the backmarkers would take him out, either by accident or on purpose. Maybe the track conditions would change, and his car would begin to slow. Maybe he would commit a silly error, giving his opponents a chance to catch him up again. Surely, he thought, something must go wrong?

It didn't. John saw his car safely round the final turn, putting his foot on the accelerator one last time to speed past the waving chequered flag.

He had done it. He was the World Champion. Nobody could ever take that away from him. He had joined the ranks of the greatest drivers in the sport.

Now the hard work would really begin. History proved that drivers did not perform well when they had the added pressure of being the reigning World Champion. Winning the World Final once was one thing, but winning it a second time was surely twice as hard.

Could he do it again?

The first set of wheels

1

Early Years

1954-1975

On 16th April 1954, Good Friday, a huge crowd brought Old Kent Road to a standstill. Local railway stations warned passengers not to alight because of the congestion. Police were summoned to shepherd the crowd and try to ensure that nobody was hurt. The streets struggled to cope with the volume of people who spilled out onto the road, stopping traffic and adding to the jam.

It was not a mass demonstration, nor a royal procession, not even an international football match. It was the pulling power of a new motorsport that had captured the imagination of public and press alike. Thousands were queuing to enter New Cross Stadium and see with their own eyes the spectacle that they had heard so much about: stock car racing.

Stock cars originated in the USA around 1947, when old roadworthy saloon cars were fitted with bumpers and roll cages and sent out to race round a track. In 1952 the sport crossed the Atlantic and stock cars raced at the Buffalo Stadium in Paris. The French organisers were keen to entertain a large crowd and the small oval tracks meant that it was difficult to overtake, so unlike the American version, drivers in Paris were encouraged to use their bumper to push and shove their opponents off the racing line. The French experiment drew enough of a crowd that others looked to replicate it elsewhere. The obvious solution was a short hop across the English Channel, and after a couple of years the arrangements were in place for the first British meeting.

Drivers were recruited by adverts in London newspapers that simply declared 'stock car drivers wanted'. Those that answered were told to seek a suitable American car, among which were Ford Model 40s, Chrysler Wimbledons and Hudson Terraplanes. Some drivers funded their own equipment, while others agreed sponsorship deals with second-hand car salesmen who would provide the car for free in return for advertising painted on the side. The glass, furnishings and upholstery were stripped out and replaced by a roll cage. An international element was provided by four French competitors, including a nobleman, Jean-Francois de Thonel, the fifth Marquis d'Orgeix. They shipped their own cars across the Channel and, as relative veterans, were the favourites to win.

Those spectators lucky enough to get into New Cross before the gates were closed were thrilled by close racing between brightly coloured cars. The stock cars roared away from the start, bumper to bumper, two abreast. Frenchman William Camus won the first race; Englishman Freddie Parson won the second. The racing was chaotic. Parson did not realise that he had won his race and continued to speed round the track. He slammed into a car that had slid sideways across the track, damaging his own vehicle and putting himself out of the rest of the meeting.

Spectacular crashes were an element of stock car racing from the start. On the first corner of one race, Jackie Voss was shunted hard into the fence, waking up in hospital with two sandbags either side of his head to stop him moving his damaged neck. Undeterred, he returned to racing as soon as he could.

He was not the only one captured by the thrill of racing. Many different drivers from varying backgrounds took to the track in the first few years. Some were rich playboys who were happy to spend their money on a hobby, others were working class mechanics for whom racing was a natural derivative from the day job. Moreover, stock car racing was not the exclusive domain of petrol-headed men. One of the sport's first stars was Tanya Crouch, a rebellious and thrill-seeking daughter of a surgeon who made a living by dynamiting tree stumps. She was a wild, unrestrained driver who pushed her car so hard that she wrecked a gearbox in her first race at the inaugural New Cross meeting. She quickly learned from her mistake and was back out on track to win the fourth race.

The press left New Cross satisfied by an interesting distraction from everyday life but sceptical of the long term viability of the sport. The public were more impressed and continued to turn out during a successful first season in which over 130 race meetings took place on more than 35 tracks. The new motorsport was able to take advantage of the many speedway and greyhound stadiums littered throughout the country and quickly built up a passionate following. The honeymoon would last until the end of the 1950s, when the entertainment became diluted by too many race meetings and crowds began to look elsewhere. That led to the first of a number of splits and schisms that would occur over the next few decades.

*

In the same year that the stock car phenomenon exploded onto the motorsport scene at New Cross, a boy was born who was destined to become the sport's greatest champion. John Lund was born in January 1954 at Colne Maternity Unit in Lancashire, the first child of a new generation in the Lund family. His father, Norman, was a dairy farmer. As was the custom of the times, he dropped off his wife Brenda at the maternity unit and returned home on the cold, frosty roads, where a couple of dozen cows needed milking. He was back a day or so later to pick up Brenda and his new son, and take them home to Smithyfold Farm at Twiston, a hamlet north of Burnley. There was no strict separation of duties in a farming family, even for a new mother. Brenda mucked in with the farm work, and would often crate up the eggs in the kitchen while rocking John's pram with her foot. Christine followed a couple of years later, a new sibling and playmate for John.

East Lancashire had survived largely unchanged for the past hundred years, seemingly unaffected by the wider world. The last cotton mills were still churning out textiles, although the steep decline in the industry was beginning to have an impact on employment levels. In the smaller villages surrounding the mill towns, farmers supplied the urban population with food. Consumption was growing as rationing finally came to an end in the UK, nearly a decade after the end of the Second World War, when the sale and purchase of meat became unrestricted in July. Farming seemed to offer a good, stable future to the men who chose it.

And a farm was a great place for an adventurous little boy to grow up. John was always on the move, climbing on the outbuildings and exploring. It started young. On one occasion, Brenda went into the barn and into the hayloft; John, still a toddler, tried to follow her up the ladder. Brenda turned around and saw him halfway up. She nearly had a heart attack. With nobody behind him and a long drop to the floor, John could have seriously injured himself if he fell.

Brenda concentrated on keeping her voice calm, trying not to panic John, and talked him up the ladder. Once he got there, he was told in no uncertain terms that he must not follow her again.

It seemed like little John had no fear. One snowy day Norman took John with him to feed the sheep on the moor. John sat on the bales of hay as Norman drove the tractor up a hill. John was told to wait with the tractor at the top; Norman did not want to take it onto the moor because of the snow. When Norman returned, John had disappeared. Thinking that he might have run home, Norman drove the tractor back to the farm. But John was not there. He turned round and drove back to the moor, finding John patiently waiting where he should have been. John had wandered off to look for a suitable place to go to the toilet, only to return and find both his dad and the tractor gone. Yet he wasn't at all upset. John just stood and waited, certain that his ride would return.

Mid-twentieth century farms tended to be small, and the Twiston farm was typical at 80 acres. However, as tractors and machinery became more common, farmers needed to be able to justify the expense of buying them. It made more sense if machines were used on larger farms, where their fixed overhead costs could be spread out more efficiently. Smaller farms merged as farmers bought or rented lots around them, taking the land of those who had retired or moved on. Norman was determined to stay, and in 1958 decided to move the family to a bigger rented farm at Rimington, four miles to the north. Wood Farm was about 150 acres, nearly double the size of Smithyfold Farm.

During the move from Twiston to Rimington, as his parents were busy packing and organising their possessions, young John was left to entertain himself. This he did by climbing onto his father's tractor and starting it up. Luckily he could not reach the pedals, and Norman rushed outside to pull his four and a half-year-old from the seat. A gleeful and proud John was taken inside to safety and better supervision. It was a hint of the future to come behind a steering wheel.

The tractor was not John's first set of wheels, however. Norman bought him those when he was just two. John used to accompany his father on trips to Burnley to buy bags of sawdust to put under the cows, and one day Norman bought John a tricycle. John was dancing a jig all the way back to the farm because he was so excited by his new toy. A day or two later Norman went to the cattle auction. John jumped on his tricycle and peddled down the road after the van. When Brenda tried to stop him, he shouted over his shoulder that he was 'going after daddy'. Perhaps it was John's racing instinct to chase a faster car!

A second daughter, Claire, was added to the Lund family at Rimington. By the time she arrived, John had started his education at Gisburn Primary School. After the eleven-plus he transferred to Clitheroe Royal Grammar School. The transition was difficult for a child who had not previously studied subjects like French and Latin, and he began to struggle academically for the first time. He was held back to repeat a year, but eventually left the school with O-Levels in English, woodwork, maths and biology. John also contributed to the French education system. The Lund family were asked to appear in a small book for French schoolchildren learning English called *This is GB: Life in a Village*. It described the life of a typical rural family, including sixteen-year-old John and his hobbies. A few months later, a letter dropped through the door addressed to 'The Lund Family, Downham, England'. Two French girls wanted to know if the Lunds were a real family, and if Downham was a real place.

It was all true, including the tale of John and his motorbike that he used to ride to school. A photograph in the book showed John with an open face helmet. Already he claimed that a full face helmet was too uncomfortable and stopped him seeing all around him, something which John would stick by right through his racing career. All the local boys were into motorbikes, and there were plenty of them around. BSA and Triumph were the badges most sought after, and could be picked up second hand for about £2.50 or £3. There was an endless carousel of trades and exchanges between friends and acquaintances. Lads would ride their bike around the fields until they tired of them and fancied a change, or saved enough money to upgrade to a better model.

John's first bike was acquired at 15 and a half, a few months before he could legally ride at 16. That time was supposed to be spent getting the bike roadworthy, since he was told it was useless. However, the 1965 Honda 125 that he bought was a good investment. The chain had broken and one of the links was trapped in the sprocket, making it feel like the engine had seized up. Pushing the heavy bike up the hill from Rimington was tough work, so John stopped to rest and put it in gear so it did not roll back down the hill. The wheels turned slightly as the slope of the hill pulled on it, which dislodged the chain link in the sprocket. Suddenly the bike felt much lighter and freer. A turn of the ignition and the engine leapt into life – it was a runner, and John had paid a fraction of the price he ought to for a bike that was only four or five years old.

That excellent first deal did not stop John from upgrading and switching his bikes as much as the other lads in the area, and he owned around ten different models in total. Riding on the roads was second best to messing around in the fields on them. John tested his mother's nerves as she stood at the kitchen sink, doing the washing up, the window in front of her looking across the farm. Suddenly John and his bike would fly up, metres in the air, as he tried to perfect his stunts on a system of ramps and jumps he had set up. Determined not to come across as a nagging mother, Brenda concentrated on the dishes, reassuring herself – not altogether successfully – that John knew what he was doing, and wouldn't hurt himself.

John did not display the speed or skill in the saddle that would later be shown in a stock car. Although he took part in one or two motocross scramble events, he had an old bike and stood no chance against more experienced riders. He would push things too hard, often damaging the bike or injuring himself. One time John limped home from an event, a big gash on his leg. It was a Sunday evening and the hospital casualty department was a long drive, so Norman took him round to the local doctor who washed and stitched the cut, but not before John completed his chores on the farm.

Life was not all play. From an early age, John helped out with farming tasks. He worked nights and weekends throughout the year and during the day in school holidays, feeding the cattle and doing the manual work required of a farmer. He was a natural at the job, but had little experience of other work and was not sure whether he wanted farming to be his life.

John never seriously considered staying on at the Grammar School to do A-Levels. Whilst he left school with O-Levels and his head held high, he realised that he did not fancy an academic future. Since he had been held back to repeat a year, his friends had already left and gone into employment. Some of them found work at an engineering plant in Clitheroe, close enough for John to walk to in his school uniform at lunchtime and after school. There John was able to tinker with the machines, picking up experience at handling steel and creating it into whatever was required.

Engineering was an appealing alternative to farming. John had taught himself the rudimentary skills needed for a successful career in engineering. Norman bought a welder for £51 from the Great Yorkshire Show in 1966, and John quickly took possession of it. Pigs were among the farm residents, and they could be very rough on the doors in the barns. John was given a load of rusty steel and tasked with reinforcing the doors so the pigs could not break them. He also built rails down the side of the barns to stop the sows crushing the piglets against the side of the barn when they clumsily lay down. It was difficult working with old, nearly-useless steel, but it gave John an opportunity to teach himself the skill of welding, and by the age of fourteen he could do more than his dad.

In order to test whether he should stick with farming or find a career in engineering, John was sent to a different farm in Kendal for a year. He was no longer working under his father and was treated like just another employee. The life of a farmer still suited him, so he returned home and began a three-year course at the Lancashire College of Agriculture at Preston. Part of the course was spent at a farm near Warrington which grew celery and lettuce on mossy soil, and while John was there the owner won a contract to supply supermarkets with boiled beetroot. John's work turned from market garden farming back to engineering as he was put to work in the sheds, welder in hand, making and installing conveyor belts to cope with the sudden increase in orders. For another part of the course John was back with more familiar livestock, but in the unfamiliar territory of a Scottish beef farm. It was a massive farm, and showed the young student how the future was being seized by big farms that could make the best use of new, modern machinery.

After finishing the course, John started working on the family farm full-time. Although dairy farming was an intensive job with long hours, the partnership between father and son gave John plenty of time to spend on hobbies. By the early 1970s, John's interest in bikes began to wane. Replacing it was a motorsport which he had come into a little contact with a few years earlier.

The first stock car that John saw belonged to Brian Wignall. John was still a pupil at Clitheroe Royal Grammar School, Brian's house and workshop was close by. The cars had moved on from that first race meeting at New Cross in 1954. In the sport's infancy, standard road cars were given big bumpers and roll cages and then sent onto the track, hence the name stock car rather than race car. During the 1960s, the cars developed from road models into custom-built cars with a fabricated, welded chassis and a race-tuned V8 engine.

The first time that he saw it, John could not mistake Brian's car for a roadworthy vehicle. Although it bore the basic shape, it had a long front bumper sticking out from the front of the car with a triangular strut on one side, and an equally strong-looking bumper at the rear. The axles stuck out from the side of the chassis so the wheels protruded half a metre from the car, and the space between them was filled with a side bumper. Brian's racing number, 102, was proudly painted on the side and on a small sheet of metal sticking up a few of inches on either side of the roof. It was obvious that this was a car used to taking contact, particularly since John regularly walked past on his way to the cricket field and saw Brian welding it back together. His interest sparked, John would call in occasionally to see what work was going on and ask a few polite questions.

Eager to see more, in 1971 John keenly accepted an invitation to join one of his friends, Alan Parker, when he travelled to Seedhill Stadium at nearby Nelson for a stock car meeting. Alan drove there on his tractor and used it to help to pull stranded cars from the stadium and back into the pits at the end of races, often with John sitting on the mudguard of the tractor. The pits were sited on the recreation ground across the main road from the stadium. In return for free entry, the local police stopped the traffic at the end of each race to allow the stock cars to trundle from the stadium back to the pits, and the next batch of cars for the next heat to cross the road into the stadium.

On the short oval track covered with a dusty shale surface, two dozen stock cars fought for position on the track. Full contact was permitted, and drivers barged cars in front of them out of the way as they entered the corners. Contact was inevitable due to the system of driver grading. Unlike most motorsports, slower drivers started at the front of the grid, the best drivers to the rear. The different grades were immediately obvious. Those at the front sported a white roof, behind them were those with yellow tops, then blue tops, with the fastest drivers in star grade sporting a red roof starting at the back. The handicap gave every driver starting the race a chance of winning, and meant that the star drivers had to use their racing skill and bumpers to chase down the front runners.

Fully immersed in the noise, action and excitement from the centre green, John was a fervent fan from the start. As long as he wasn't at a distant college placement, John would join Alan at Nelson on a Saturday evening. There he viewed many of the top names in the sport, some of whom would influence John's future racing style. Prominent among these were Doug Cronshaw and Stuart Smith. They started racing together in the mid-1960s and formed a partnership, even sharing a car, until they had enough experience and expertise to go their separate ways and race alone. Since they were based in Rochdale, just twenty miles away, both Cronshaw and Smith were regulars at Nelson.

Cronshaw was initially the more successful of the two; winning his first meeting final in 1967. He had a Pontiac-powered car which was underpowered compared to many of his competitors, but what he lacked in power, he made up for with flair. He would pass cars through the smallest of gaps where most of the other drivers wouldn't be able to. He used his own racing line on the shale surface, putting the car sideways halfway down the straight to prepare for the corner, keeping the engine revs up and momentum and speed right through the corner. Other drivers with more power could drive into the bend and use their power to accelerate out. When he fitted his car with a Chevrolet engine Cronshaw became more competitive. His signature driving-style on shale remained, as did his ability to pass other cars in seemingly impossible situations, and he drove to the World Championship title in 1971. Cronshaw quickly became John's favourite driver, somebody who John would later hope to emulate.

Despite Cronshaw's flair, Stuart Smith soon became the man to beat. He won the World Final in 1972 and finished second for the next three years. He was also the winner of the National Points Championship every season after 1969, a testament to his consistent racing results and ability to turn out his car at many different meetings throughout the season.

In comparison to Cronshaw, who seemed to weasel his way through a compact field, Smith seemed to glide through it, other drivers appearing to let him pass as soon as they caught a glimpse of number 391 in their mirrors. John watched on the sidelines, wondering why drivers made it easy for him. Like many others both before and after him, John decided that if he were racing, he would not make it so easy for any car behind him. It took a few years for John to realise that Smith's real skill was to control his car so he made it look easy.

Stock cars raced at Nelson every three weeks or so during the racing season which ran from March to November. On the intervening weekends Seedhill Stadium hosted banger racing and hell cars. The hell cars were a standard road car with extra armour welded onto it, a formula of racing much closer to the original stock cars of 1954. Rover 90s were a favourite because they were already very strong, but a number of Ford Anglias and Ford Populars made an appearance too.

Alan Parker had a brief career racing in hell cars, but found himself on the sidelines for breaking the regulations by putting a Jaguar engine into a Ford body. That didn't stop a friend borrowing the car to race it himself with a new paint job, and he was lucky enough that he was not found out. Unable to race, Alan decided that he wanted to take a step up the racing ladder and begin racing stock cars.

Building a stock car from scratch was not an undertaking for the faint-hearted, and Alan sought the support of his friends. John was quick to offer his backing. The idea of building a stock car appealed to the man who had spent his teenage years on farms, messing around with steel and various bits of farming equipment, teaching himself to weld. John had seen stock cars up close as they were towed from the track by Alan's tractor and thought that he could have a good go at building one. The opportunity to work with new, fresh steel rather than rusty leftovers to build pig pens was also a contributing factor in John's enthusiasm.

Alan planned their project. A small group of friends gathered in his workshop: Alan, John, Dave Seed, George Braithwaite, and a second John Lund – this one from Gisburn, no relation to the other John, and four years younger. They were a band of young motorsport enthusiasts, and eventually all five would build and race stock cars.

Under Alan's direction the basic shape of the stock car took shape. The flat chassis was laid out and welded together, and the engine plate added. Unfortunately, work was slow. Not only had none of them built a car from scratch before, but Alan was distracted. Each session they spent on the car it would seem like they were making progress, but then Alan's eyes would light up as he heard the clip-clop of an approaching horse. It was not the animal that interested him, but the rider. Alan's relationship with a local girl who lived on the other side of the river was beginning to blossom, and each time she came to see him work finished for the day. As his interest in her grew, his interest in the car subsided.

That left a largely incomplete car, but the stock car bug had bitten John. He had time to devote to the sport, and bits and pieces of old cars soon found their way to Wood Farm. The welding kit John requested for his 21st birthday came into its own in building a new chassis. Suspension and roll cage were added to the chassis, axles from a Morris Commercial were welded in place, and a Buick engine was lowered inside. Once the body panels and bumpers were added, the unique appearance of a stock car was unveiled.

Work began in September 1976 and was completed a few months later. With Alan no longer interested, there was nobody to drive it. So John made a decision that had a massive impact on both his future, and that of the sport: he had built the car, why not drive it?

Ready to race

2

Novice

1976

Sunday 28th March 1976 was the first warm day of spring, reaching 17 degrees in some places. The pleasant heat sent families out in droves to enjoy Mother's Day. They were not able to go to the Ideal Home Exhibition at the Olympia centre in London, which was closed after an IRA bomb exploded the previous day, injuring 70 people, four of whom had to have limbs amputated. The country was waiting to see who would be the next Prime Minister after Harold Wilson surprisingly announced his retirement. Labour MPs were preparing for the second ballot to decide the next occupant of Downing Street, a three-way race between Jim Callaghan, Michael Foot and Denis Healey. Queens Park Rangers led English football's First Division by one point from Manchester United and Derby County. Ferrari gained a one-two in the United States Grand Prix; Clay Regazzoni of Switzerland brought his car home ahead of World Champion Niki Lauda.

John Lund ignored all these distractions as he nervously prepared his stock car for its first appearance at a race meeting. The venue was the Athletic Ground in Rochdale, home of the Rochdale Hornets rugby league team. A track around the rugby pitch had formerly been used for greyhound racing and speedway but was now the sole preserve of stock cars. It was a tricky oval to negotiate. On the outside, a steel wire fence supported by steel uprights was ready to tear off an outside wheel. On the inside, high kerbstones could damage tyres and wheels.

John's nerves were not helped by the fact that he was drawn in the third and final heat, so he had to wait through two races before he got out on the track. Brian Wallace took the chequered flag in the first race, while the ever-reliable Doug Cronshaw won the second. As the shale dust settled and the cars were cleared from the track, John trundled out from the pits in his new silver-bodied car and across the public highway for his debut race.

A white roof signified that John was in the lowest grade of racing, but he did not start at the front with the other white tops. A prominent black cross on the back of his car, the stock car equivalent of L-plates, warned other drivers that he was a novice in one of his first races. This allowed John to start at the very back of the grid, giving him a few moments to get used to driving round the track before the rest of the field made up the half-lap and overtook him. Gordon Smith was a star driver with a red roof and started just in front of John at the back of the regular grid. Dave Berresford, an upcoming driver who was tipped as a potential champion, was also towards the back. The cars crawled around the track at walking pace for the rolling lap. Drivers jostled for position, some dropping back to give themselves a bit of space, others bunching close to the rear bumper of the car in front, all varying their pace to try and to the best start.

The green flag waved and John's racing career began. Almost immediately the reality of stock car racing hit. Whereas John was not so naïve that he expected to fly around the track at the same speed as his opponents, what he did not realise was that getting round a lap would be so difficult. Press the accelerator down hard, the kind of pressure that was needed to get anywhere near racing pace, and the car seemed to develop a life of its own. Before long John had spun the car and was facing the wrong way. Pretty much the entire field flew past in a cacophony of thundering exhausts, a hail of shale splattering the car. There was no damage – John's car had not been touched – so he found the right direction and set off again. Unfortunately, it was a matter of seconds before he spun again. Regardless of the other cars, John was finding it difficult to maintain speed and direction; he could manage one at a time, but not both. Add into the mix the other cars, who nudged and shoved John whenever he found himself in their way, and driving seemed impossible. John seemed to spend more of the race facing the wrong way than the right one.

The racing continued around him. An incident on one part of the track meant that most of it was blocked. There was a narrow gap to squeeze through, and a few cars made it. Those that were unlucky, or who were forced out by their opponents, joined the pile up. John careered towards the stranded cars, barely in control of his own. The result seemed inevitable, yet John squeezed through the narrow gap and continued on. The pile up meant that there were now far fewer competitors racing on the track.

John continued to negotiate the small gap in the carnage which gradually opened up as damaged cars limped onto the centre green. Unsurprisingly the best drivers had avoided trouble and cruised to the finish. The chequered flag was waved to Gordon

Smith; Dave Berresford finished behind him. What was more surprising was that John Lund, the novice starting his first race, had completed it and finished seventh. True, he was a distant seventh. True, there were no other finishers behind him. But the difficult first race was now under his belt.

Seventh was not enough to qualify for the final, only the top six made it. He lined up at the back of the grid again in the consolation, a race which gave drivers who did not qualify from their heat a second chance to make the final. John still struggled to control his car and fought a continual battle with the controls while the rest of the field raced past him. Eventually he retired to the safety of the centre green, his car finally having had enough of the rough treatment John had given it.

Watching from the sidelines, the meeting final was a whole other world. Instead of a grid comprising a mix of drivers from all grades, this time there were few white and yellow tops in a field dominated by blue and red roofs. At the back of the grid sat Doug Cronshaw and Frankie Wainman, two of the top names in the sport who had gained one of the slots in the new superstar grading that allowed the driver to carry flashing amber lights under his red roof. In front of them, the star grade drivers with red roofs included Mike Close, Gordon Smith and Brian Wallace. Wainman won the final, followed by Close and Wallace. John came back out for the Grand National, his last start as a novice at the back of the grid, but did not stay out on track for long. Cronshaw won the Grand National, with Wallace capping off a good meeting in second; he had raced three times and finished each in the top three. John, the young novice, was far off the pace and an irrelevance in each of his three races, although his multiple spins did provide great entertainment for the spectators.

*

Nevertheless, it was an achievement that John was out on track at all. He completed his car build in a matter of months, a largely solo effort helped by a few local friends and drivers. Brian Wignall and Henry Wolfenden were locals and allowed John to measure up their cars, but John wanted to do more than just copy what he saw. Looking around the pits for inspiration, John had identified two main car builders, John Hillam and Allan Barker. Both used different designs, but John thought that both had their flaws. The main problem was the structure of the chassis and how it affected the frontal strength of the cars. Hillam's cars had a chassis formed with a square cross, giving it good all-round strength, but if he hit somebody head-on, right in the middle of the bumper, it could bend the chassis straight back. Barker's chassis frame was less square and more v-shaped, angling towards the front of the car. That gave better strength for a head-on impact, but it didn't take much force to twist the chassis out of shape. John chose to try his own chassis shape, laying down two cross-rails and adding cross-braces for support and strength. He also used steel with a smaller section for greater strength, hoping that it would give the chassis greater ability to withstand impacts.

Over the winter of 1975-76, John applied for a racing licence. When it returned, he found that he had been randomly designated a free number: 53. That number, which would become inextricably linked to John in the future, had previously been used by a number of different drivers. During the 1960s it was used on cars in three short-lived racing careers: Henry Nakarno, Ian Gilbertson and Ron Parkin. In 1967 the number 53 found a more lasting home when Ian Barker raced under it for eight years. Barker retired from racing at the end of the 1975 season, and the number was freed for the next driver to apply for a licence.

John painted the number 53 on his car and contacted Mike Parker to request a slot at the first stock car meeting of the season at Nelson on 20th March. Parker was a significant and powerful player in the stock car world. A former driver from the earliest days of the sport in the 1950s, he branched out into promoting meetings for stock cars, speedway and other motorsport formulas during the 1960s. By the 1976 season he was organising and promoting 50 of 160 stock car meetings, at Nelson, Rochdale, Stoke and White City in Manchester. John was told that the first Nelson meeting of the season was full, so transferred to the Rochdale date eight days later.

John belatedly made it to Nelson at his second meeting, the Friday following his Rochdale debut, but found that the new track did little to improve his control. Another shale surface, too often he would lose traction and spin round, costing him valuable time and giving him no chance to keep up with the front runners. He crashed out of the heat and final, but kept his car on the track for long enough in the consolation to claim third place behind Alan Scothern and George Stringer. A podium finish in only his second meeting was a great achievement.

Similarly to Rochdale, the Nelson meeting indicated that there were flashes of a potentially decent driver struggling in a wayward car. The trouble was that the other drivers were secretive about their car setup and volunteered very little advice. John's only options were to glean what he could by sight in the pits, but that only meant that he could look at obvious external features – anything under the bonnet or behind panelling was off-limits – and to tinker with his own car, experimenting to see how different setups affected racing. If it didn't work, he would have another look around the pits and try again.

The experimentation process was slow. John returned from thirteen consecutive meetings with a bent front axle. He was pushing his car beyond its limits, yet still could not get the car to turn into corners well. Eventually a mechanic for Ron Cotterill, a yellow top who John had a habit of taking out by accident in his fight to control his own car, approached John in the pits. The mechanic's advice, given to protect his own driver rather than to help John, was to lean back the front axle and put some wedges under the springs to stop the car spinning. Other than that small bit of advice, John was on his own.

Those first few months were a struggle. John's biggest problem was that he did not know how to stagger the car to get the best turn through the corners. The car was going round an oval circuit, only turning left. This meant that the car should have been set up to improve turning ability to that side, even if it harmed right-turning capability – that direction just did not matter. In his first few meetings, John was using the same size wheels on both sides of the car. Soon he realised that he could put slightly bigger wheels on the outside to aid cornering. Gradually he managed to improve his setup so he could take corners at greater speed without spinning. Nevertheless, the slow process of crashing and righting himself taught John some valuable lessons, not the least of which was how to get out of some sticky situations.

Struggling with an incorrect setup meant that John was unable to sneak through the small gaps that appeared on track as his opponents got it wrong. Labouring away, John relied on the only technique he had to get past those around him: he forced his way through. Stock car racing is a motorsport in which full contact racing is allowed, so John was well within his rights to do this. Only dangerous driving was banned, which meant that a driver had to make an effort to follow the race track and could not smash an opponent into the fence at the end of the straight at full speed.

Full contact racing involves a great deal of skill, more than just hitting the car in front. Contact needs to be timed so that when the driver of a car enters a turn, he brakes late and uses the car in front to reduce speed. Momentum is passed onto his opponent who is forced wide, allowing the driver who initiated the contact to pass on the inside. Of course, it also means that the car pushed wide is now in a position to perform exactly the same manoeuvre on the next turn because they have a wider line and can accelerate out of the corner sooner.

However, racing is rarely so simple, and drivers are often able to shove cars with enough force that they are pushed into another car further ahead, much like a snooker player cannons a ball off another, meaning that stock cars can pass multiple opponents in one corner. Drivers may also deliberately aim to shove the car in front into a stranded car or pack of cars, effectively blocking the path of their opponent and causing them to take evasive action. Yet the use of the bumper can very easily go wrong. Rather than spinning or sending an opponent into the fence, a misplaced or mistimed hit can cause grief to an attacking driver, leaving them facing the wrong way or in the fence.

In a car that did not respond or corner as he hoped it would, John's use of the bumper was fairly basic in his initial races and he quickly gained a reputation as a maverick driver who was willing to risk damage to his own car in clumsy overtaking attempts. Too often he was the one who hit the fence rather than his opponents.

Typical of John's early approach to racing was an encounter with Ray Leigh at Nelson. Leigh had knocked John out of a few races, and after one heat a frustrated and angry John was towed to the pits by a tractor; a rear axle hanging off after another hit from Leigh caused John to clip the fence with his outside wheel. It looked like John's evening was over, and his mechanics asked if they should pack up the car. 'No,' came the reply, 'I'm going to bury Ray Leigh.' And bury him he did. John worked on the car to get it fit for the Grand National and spent the race looking to get into position just behind Leigh. Then he left his foot on the accelerator and launched his car forward, shoving Leigh hard into the fence, leaving him dangling on the steel ropes.

John would also go to watch and pick up a few tips when he was not racing. One such meeting was held on 5th June at White City Stadium in Manchester. John spent the day on the farm, and once work was complete he jumped in the car with a couple of friends and set off to Manchester, hoping to catch the end of the meeting. When he got there, he began to doubt that he had turned up on the right evening. The car park was busy, but there was no sound coming from the stadium; no engines running, nor the usual hubbub of a Saturday night stock car crowd. Walking into the pits, John found that there were many stock cars parked up, but no drivers were ready, and there was a sombre, muted atmosphere.

John had arrived a few minutes after an accident claimed the life of Brian Wallace, a red top driver who had raced at all nine meetings that John had so far attended in his short career. In the Grand National, the last race of the evening, Wallace's throttle had jammed and he slammed head-on into the fence at the end of one of the straights. The front of the car ploughed through the fence and one of the steel wires cut through the roll cage bars at the front of the cab, pinning Wallace to his seat. The pressure caused massive internal damage in his chest and his death was almost immediate.

Although it was the first fatality in stock car racing for years, it was a reminder of the risks that drivers took. Further heartbreak came in the following month, when Tony Abel, a Midlands-based white top driver, became entangled in the home straight at Northampton. While Abel waited for a safe moment to exit the car, another car hit him from behind at full speed. The massive jolt caused serious spinal injuries and left Abel permanently paralysed.

Many young drivers making their first foray into motorsport might have had second thoughts after two bad accidents in quick succession. Considering that cars could be brought to an almost immediate halt from speeds of 60 miles per hour, injuries and fatalities were almost inevitable. Over the space of a few weeks, one driver had been killed and another was so seriously injured that it would affect the rest of his life. Moreover, it could happen to any driver; Wallace was one of the best, Abel was just starting out. However, John was determined to carry on racing. His was the attitude that drivers need to have – he never thought it would happen to him. Like all stock cars drivers, he continued climbing into his self-built car which was designed with fairly minimal rules and regulations about protection and bracing.

Just as he was not racing when Brian Wallace died, John did not attend the meeting where Tony Abel was paralysed. The first thirteen race meetings he attended were at three different tracks: Rochdale, Nelson and Bradford. He had a good record of qualifying for the meeting final with regular finishes between fourth and eighth in heats and consolations. A glimpse of talent was seen in the last weekend of May, when John finished second in two consecutive heats; first at Nelson on Saturday, then at Rochdale on Sunday. But John found the step up in standard in the finals too much to cope with and he did not finish a single one. Moreover, the stress placed on his car by an incorrect setup meant that he finished each meeting with a bent front axle.

In his opening season, John came up against the gold roof of the World Champion on one occasion only. Dave Chisholm had won the 1975 World Final, making him the first driver in the history of the sport to win three consecutive World Championships. On the opening meeting of the 1976 season, at Northampton on 14th March, Chisholm injured his back in a crash. He spent two months recovering and returned to racing in mid-May. His third meeting back, on 27th May, was at Bradford, the third time that John had raced across the Pennines in West Yorkshire. Chisholm started at the back of heat 2, with John at the front. Positions were reversed by the end of the race, with Chisholm taking the chequered flag first and John crossing the line in eighth. Both cars turned out for the final (John had to finish fifth in the consolation to get there) but neither finished in the top eight.

John branched out from his three familiar tracks in mid-July, and with some success. On Saturday 17th July he travelled the short distance to White City and raced for the first time on tarmac. White City had been given a new surface at the start of 1976, having previously been another shale track, and tarmac necessitated a very different driving style. Cars had more grip, enabling them to accelerate and brake more rapidly. Cornering required a different technique with less sliding, and cars could travel through the corners at higher speed, although the short straights at White City meant that extra speed out of corners was not so valuable. John finished seventh in his heat but did not finish in his other races.

The following day John travelled up to Aycliffe, just north of Darlington, for another tarmac meeting. Learning quickly from his experiences the previous day, John managed to squeeze into the meeting final by finishing sixth in his heat. That meant he found himself at the front of the grid with a host of red top cars behind him, each fighting to get past and claim the win for themselves. This time John was able to shepherd his car through the race, avoiding the usual shunts from behind, keeping his car out of trouble, and passing the starter to finish the race. Willie Harrison won, joined on the podium by Stuart Smith and Mike Close. Stuart Bamforth and Sam Ostle next came in, followed by John in sixth. It was his first meeting final finish, and another sign that the young John was learning both how to set up his car and race it on the track.

Regular race finishes meant that John moved away from the front of the grid, swapping his white roof for a yellow one. That still put him among the first few rows, but now dangerously close to the blue tops, more experienced drivers who could wallop a rival into the fence in the first corners as they strove to escape from their tightly-packed opponents at the start of the race. Nevertheless, John continued to grind out results from his new grading, finishing in the top eight but off the podium in the heats and consolation at Rochdale, Nelson, Bradford and White City. More final finishes were too much to ask for. John was still struggling to shepherd his car through complete meetings, a combination of incorrect setup and his own aggressive driving style. Too often more experienced drivers despatched him into the fence or mechanical failures despatched him to the centre green.

As he slowly clawed his way up the grading list, John decided to make his first long-distance trip to a meeting in the south. The tarmac Race of Champions, hosted by Brafield Stadium at Northampton, offered slightly different qualification arrangements for the meeting final. Each driver raced in one of four heats and those who were unsuccessful had a second opportunity in one of two consolation heats. Drivers who qualified from the heats then raced in one of two semi-finals, with a consolation semi-final for those who did not qualify at the first time of asking. The results of the semi-finals determined the grid for the meeting final.

The technicalities of qualification passed John by, however, as he failed to finish in either his heat or consolation and failed to progress. The 175 mile journey back to Rimington from Northampton, pulling the stock car on a trailer behind a Landrover, was a slow one. It gave John plenty of time to think about the future. He had shown that he could get regular finishes in the top eight in heats. He could even, when conditions favoured him, sneak onto the podium. However, he was not yet able to compete with the best drivers in meeting finals, and was nowhere near challenging the red tops. Something was still missing.

Perhaps all that he needed was a stroke of luck. The following Friday evening, John returned to the familiar shale of Nelson. Many of the best drivers were allocated the third heat, which doubled up as a semi-final for the Driver of the Year championship held on the four Mike Parker Promotion tracks. Among them was John, and he failed to make the top eight in a field that boasted Stuart Smith, Willie Harrison, John Hillam and Mike Close. The inferior fields in heats 1 and 2 should have given the drivers in them a good chance of qualifying for the final, but tracks conditions meant that only seven cars finished in the first heat and six in the second. So it was a packed grid of drivers that formed up for the consolation race, among whom was John.

Starting from yellow top gave John an advantage. There were a number of red tops, mostly leftovers who had failed to finish the Driver of the Year semi-final, but in their haste and desperation to qualify for the meeting final they held each other up. That gave John the luxury of extra time before the pressure came on from behind, and he slowly worked away from the yellow tops, through the white tops into the lead. The red tops inevitably began to draw him in, superstar John Hillam leading the chase, but the gap between them was too wide. John held off Hillam to pass a waving chequered flag for his first race victory. He celebrated back in the pits, but was soon back out on track for the meeting final. Normal service resumed: John did not finish after rolling his car onto its roof!

John went to Rochdale the following day, where the second Parker Promotions Driver of the Year semi-final doubled up as heat 3 and drew off many of the better drivers. Having already raced in the first semi-final the day before, John went on track in the first heat with a reduced grid. Once again he started among the yellow tops, and once again he pushed clear of the yellows and through the whites into the lead. This time the pressure from the red tops never materialised, and John took his second ever race victory – and second in two days – with Malcolm Dobson and John Stirk trailing in behind.

Little had changed from the failure at Northampton other than John had been fortuitous in the Driver of the Year semi-finals giving him favourable grids to race in. However, the two race victories gave him a new confidence and belief in his car setup and ability. John managed his second ever finish in the final at the Rochdale meeting in which he won the heat. Doug Cronshaw took the final victory, this time Malcolm Dobson got past for second, but John hung on for third and his first podium finish in a meeting final. As if that were not enough, he also finished third in the Grand National. Doug Cronshaw came back from the one lap-down disadvantage that the winner of a meeting final carries into the Grand National and worked his way right through the field to take the chequered flag. Mike Close pushed past John for second, but John took his place on the third step of the podium for the second time that night.

Eight days later, back at Rochdale, John was back on the podium again, with third place in his heat. The flurry of podium places meant that John had a repainting job to do when the new grading list was published at the end of the month. He had progressed to blue top, only one grade in front of the red-roofed star drivers. Now he would have very little time to get round the track before the stars would be on his back bumper, fighting to get past him. As if that were not bad enough, a little further back were the superstar drivers who started at the back of the red tops; Stuart Smith, Willie Harrison, Frankie Wainman, Doug Cronshaw, John Hillam and Mike Close.

If there was extra pressure on John, it didn't show. The first three meetings in October saw him qualify for and finish sixth in each final, twice at Nelson and once at White City. John was more than holding his own at blue top. He found that the first person to run into the back of his car at the start of the race would usually be Dave Beresford, with Gordon Smith close behind. There was no point in trying to stop them banging his car wide, otherwise they would get frustrated and hit the back bumper so hard that John would slide into the fence. Instead he rode the hit, giving Berresford and Smith a gap to sneak down the inside but then getting back behind them before any others could get through. This then gave John the opportunity to follow Berresford and Smith round the track, often benefiting as they scythed through the field, and by the time the superstars were on his back bumper the track had opened out a little and their hits were less dangerous.

John's first appearance on track had been at Rochdale, so it was fitting that seven months later, on 10th October, it was also the site of John's first meeting final win. Having qualified from the third heat in second place, John knew that his car was running well. He started the final, as always, expecting a nudge from Berresford and Smith in the first lap or two. This time, however, it never came. John edged ahead of his fellow blue tops and through the yellows and whites in front of him. Still the challenge from behind did not appear, and only by the last few laps did Rod Falding work clear of the chasing pack and get close. Were the race to have been extended by another five laps, Falding would have probably been able to push past and claim the win. But John had time on his side, and held off Falding to take the chequered flag, his third race victory and first in a final.

It was the high point of an excellent month. John now entered the Grand National race at the end of the Rochdale meeting and as the final winner started a lap down, just in front of the white tops. Yet he still made his way through the much of the field, finishing in a creditable eighth place. Five days later, John travelled to Nelson. He again benefited from the Driver of the Year competition, the final of which drew off some of the better drivers from the first heat. John sped to victory, pursued by Stuart Bamforth and Jack Ollerenshaw. He finished the meeting final in eighth but picked up a second race win in the Grand National, this time finishing in front of Mike Close, Doug Cronshaw, Willie Harrison and Dave Berresford. The next day saw two third places at Rochdale, in the consolation and final.

With his first season drawing to a close, John was left with one major commitment to fulfil: the Novice of the Year race, an annual championship open to all drivers who had begun racing for the first time during the 1976 season. The venue of the race, Rochdale, meant that John entered the race as favourite. He had already raced there ten times during the season and won a meeting final. His main rival for the title was Andy Stott, who was making his sixth appearance at Rochdale. Stott started driving two months after John but travelled more widely, attending double the number of meetings that John did. Regular finishes in the top eight, including two victories in consolations, meant that Stott rose through the grading list alongside John, and the two often found themselves next to each other on the grid.

In line with most predictions, it was a two-car race. John and Stott opened up a lead on the other novice drivers, many of whom were still sporting white and yellow roofs. As usual, John drifted round the Rochdale corners sideways, splattering the windows of the grandstand bar with shale. Stott had raced on enough shale tracks to pick up the cornering technique too, and took the lead.

The sideways power slide was the fastest way of circling Rochdale, but a car going into the corner with a slightly wrong line could catch the fence with its outside rear tyre. John did exactly that, and knocked the fence. His axle was undamaged but the tyre soon lost the air in it, although it was close enough to the end of the race that John still managed to get across the line with a flat tyre. Stott held onto his lead to finish the race first; John was behind him in second.

There was no real surprise in the result. Both drivers were equally matched, and the small advantage that John had in the venue and his prior final victory there was compensated for by Stott's racing experience picked up in the greater number of meetings he had attended. Brian Whorton, a Midlands-based driver who had yet to reach double figures in terms of meetings attended, finished a creditable third.

The season drifted to an end with November meetings at White City and Rochdale. John reflected on a good first year. True, he had a reputation as a bruising racer, a driver who could put his bumper into the back of an opponent and see them into the fence, but also somebody who was just as likely to trash his own car through an ill-timed and poorly-thought manoeuvre. Yet John also illustrated that he had skill and ability lurking underneath the surface. He was sitting in the middle of blue grade and was tipped as a safe bet for a red top in the future. Some drivers had taken years to rise to a position in the grading list that John now held. The next task was to build on a solid foundation and fulfil his obvious potential.

Waiting for the green flag at Belle Vue, 1977

3

Star

1977-1980

John was not concerned whether people in the sport viewed him as a future red top or a potential champion. Every time he went on track, he had one aim only: to win races. Whether it was a World Final or a meeting consolation, it didn't matter. That simple aim stayed with John throughout his career, from 1976 through to the second decade of the 21st century, and has surely contributed to his remarkable longevity in the sport.

Of course, at the dawn of his second season in stock car racing, John had won only a single meeting final and four other races. He came pretty close to adding a second meeting final in three consecutive meetings: at White City in the New Year Trophy meeting on 1st January, also at the first regular season White City meeting on 19th March and at Sheffield on 21st March. On each occasion John finished second to Stuart Smith.

Being beaten by Smith was nothing to be ashamed of. The Sheffield victory was his 286th final win, a total far greater than anyone else in the sport, and he had just completed his best season for meeting finals, 1976, during which he passed the chequered flag first 55 times. Smith churned out victories with such regularity that no other driver could hope to match him. Only the World Championship seemed to evade him. He had won it twice, in 1969 and 1972, but that did not seem enough for such a dominant driver. Three consecutive second place finishes to Dave Chisholm between 1973 and 1975 were frustrating, but not as much as the 1976 World Final, which Smith did not even start. Having crashed out of the World Semi-Final at Coventry, Smith could only watch from the sidelines while Stuart Bamforth cruised through to victory as those in front of him took each other out of the race.

Nevertheless, despite his World Final disappointment Smith enjoyed so much success that he was able to fund his racing entirely through profits earned by winning meetings. He travelled to the far ends of the country, from Bristol to Hartlepool, taking in every track in between. Aside from merely ploughing money into the 391 car, Smith was also one of the sport's greatest innovators. The 1976 car that brought him so much success was nicknamed the Dodo after the small wings on the roof designed to help the car corner. It was one of the first attempts to improve the aerodynamics on a stock car and it was typical of Smith's thoughtful approach to car construction. Coupled with unparalleled race craft, car control and deft bumper work, Smith often seemed unbeatable.

John was never one to be blinded by reputations. He vowed that he would never easily allow Smith past, and the promise was honoured. Each time Smith had to work for his victory; John would not merely move out of the way and settle for second place. The closest he came to holding off Smith was at Sheffield, where he held the lead with two laps to go on a rough track. Smith managed to manoeuvre his way past, however, and once he had the lead could open up enough of a gap to prevent John trying a last-bend wallop.

John's impressive start to the 1977 season was due to a major change in his car. He had raced in 1976 with a Buick engine re-built from the remains of two damaged ones; one purchased from fellow Lancastrian driver Harry Smith, and one from retired racer Bill Houseman who ran a scrap yard in North Yorkshire. John resurrected one of the engines and was left with enough spares parts to make up half of another engine. The working engine ran fine until about halfway through the first season, when it blew up at White City. John was now forced into another rebuild, this time with only a week or so before his next meeting. Using what he could salvage from the engine that gave up at White City and the spares he already had in hand, John was able to get one engine running. That saw him through to the end of the season, but it was clear that he would need to invest in a new power unit.

The Buick engines were generally reliable at grimy shale tracks like Nelson and Rochdale. Both car and driver would leave the track covered in wet dust, and it seemed like more time was spent washing the car after meetings than doing mechanical repairs. John drove his car into the farm yard and left it running while he power-washed it, even aiming the water jet at the spark plugs and distributor. The Buick never missed a beat. It was the same on the racetrack, never faltering even in the dirtiest of conditions; the Buick would keep going while others were misfiring.

However, John felt that he was far off the pace on tarmac tracks like White City. There his Buick lacked power and his opponents were able to simply drive away from him with their greater speed. More and more drivers were racing with Chevrolet engines. If John had a Chevy too it would give him more power and a greater ability to compete with the top drivers on tarmac tracks.

John mentioned that he was thinking of changing engines to Brian Wignall, who had virtually retired by this point and was happy to offer suggestions to the young driver who had visited his workshop since his schooldays. Wignall's advice was clear; a Chevrolet was the only way to compete on tarmac. John made a few enquiries and found out that Ernie Hatton, a scrap yard owner who had stopped racing halfway through the 1976 season, was looking to offload his equipment. John did not have much to spend and initially looked at a spare Chevrolet that was in bits. He then asked Hatton if he could look at the engine in his race car as well. He removed the sump and found out that the bearings inside were damaged and would require repair. Hatton was not interested in doing the work, so John made him an offer for the engine and car. Having initially gone to look at an engine in pieces, John came away with a complete engine and stock car for a knock-down price. The choice to move to Chevys was sealed, so John sold his Buick and modified his car to take the new engine. Hatton's old car was retained for spare parts.

It was largely because of the new Chevrolet in his car that John started 1977 so impressively. Aside from his three consecutive second places in finals, he also finished second or third in ten heats or Grand Nationals in March and April. The same months saw John extend his racing commitments, travelling to Long Eaton and Hartlepool for the first time, as well as Sheffield and Manchester's Belle Vue, where John had first appeared in the Christmas meetings. More races and some impressive placings meant more points, and in the first new grading list of 1977 John was promoted to star grade. He could now wear the red roof that signified the best drivers on the grid, and would hold star grade or above for the next three decades.

Of course, the new Chevrolet engine was not perfect. Throughout July a leaky radiator caused it to overheat. John's solution was to crack a couple of eggs and pour them into the radiator; the heat caused the eggs to harden and seal the hole. The unusual solution worked fairly well until John came to race in his first World Championship Semi-Final at Long Eaton on 30th July.

Qualification for the World Semi-Finals depended on points picked up in designated qualifying rounds throughout the season. In his first season, John did not get enough points to make it to a semi. In 1977, John appeared in five qualifying rounds but only managed to finish the final at two of them, fourth at Rochdale and ninth at Skegness. That left him a disappointing 25th in the qualification points list and meant that he was designated a grid position on the seventh row in the Long Eaton World Semi-Final.

John had plenty of work to do if he was to be one of the top ten finishers who qualified for the World Final. Unusually in stock car racing, the better drivers started at the front of the grid, and John would need to pass at least three of them. While Frankie Wainman and Dave Hodgson drove off from the comfort of the front row, maintaining their position until the end of the race, John was caught up in a mid-grid scrap that culminated in him rolling onto his roof. Waved yellow flags brought racing to a temporary halt while his car was turned back onto its wheels, but John was out of the race and out of the quest for the World Championship. To add insult to injury, the rollover blew the top hose on the engine and covered John in stinking rotten egg water.

Rollovers may look spectacular, but damage sustained in them is often cosmetic rather than mechanical. Although John did not race for the remainder of the Long Eaton meeting, he was back on track the following day for his only career appearance at Brands

Hatch, in the Festival of Speed. A small meeting of five races saw John qualify for the final from fifth in the consolation and finish fourth in the Grand National.

Although he had not qualified for the World Final, John was able to take in the atmosphere of the biggest stock car meeting of the year when he travelled to Coventry to take part in the rest of the meeting. As a non-qualifier for the main event, John found himself out on track for the first of two regular meeting heats, while the World Final doubled up as heat 3. With most of the best drivers in the World Final, John took advantage of the depleted field and came home first, ahead of Bernard Poyser and Danny Clarke. Mike Close won the World Final from Frankie Wainman, having taken the lead with five laps to go.

The heat win at the World Championship meeting was not John's only success of the season. He also won three races at Rochdale, two at Nelson and Sheffield, and one at White City and Aycliffe. All were heats, consolations or Grand Nationals; a second meeting final victory would have to wait until the end of 1978.

It was Rochdale that was the scene for meeting final success again, on 7th October 1978. True, John benefited from a low turn out of cars, a sign that Rochdale was struggling to draw sufficient numbers of drivers. Part of the trouble was that different venues often held meetings on the same evening, and on this occasion some drivers, including Stuart Smith, opted to travel down to Coventry rather than race at Rochdale. That was not the only reason for Rochdale's struggles, however, because later in the month Rochdale held a solus event with no clashing fixtures and still only found enough entries for two heats instead of the more customary three.

Nevertheless, John still had to hold off Frankie Wainman, Mike Close, Gordon Smith and Dave Berresford with a steady drive in slippery conditions to win the meeting final. It was two years since John's inaugural final win and as he went round the final bend he gave the accelerator a heavy stomp to go over the line in triumph. After taking the chequered flag he cruised into the turn at the end of the home straight, but a disturbing rattle suddenly emanated from under the bonnet. The car limped back to the pits, the noise getting worse. A threaded bar that held the air cleaner in place had broken and got into the engine. When John put his pedal to the metal on the last bend, the secondaries on the carburettor opened a little bit more and bent a valve. Had he pressed down hard with a couple of laps to go rather than the last bend, it is likely he would not have made it to the line.

Why had it taken so long for John to claim a second final victory? Since progressing to star grade at the start of 1977 John had to start at the back of the grid. From there he was able to get to the top eight, often the podium, but found it difficult to win races. Each time he got close it seemed that one of the top men sneaked past, or one of the lower grade drivers managed to break free and build up too great a lead.

Nevertheless, the process of tinkering with the car setup continued and John slowly but steadily built up a bank of racing experience that he would be able to call on in later years. Unlike his volatile first season, John was learning how to keep out of trouble on the track. With less damage requiring repair at the end of each meeting, John was able to concentrate on improving what he already had. His first car lasted two seasons, but over the winter before the 1978 season John built a new one. The old car was sold to Gary Murray and would last a good few seasons yet.

The new Lund car was broadly similar in shape and specification to the first, but an angular square cab and distinctive forward-leaning front made the car recognisable on track. Aesthetics aside, an improvement to the suspension saw John ditch the old leaf springs that he had been using and fit quarter elliptics, the kind of suspension that Mike Close, Stuart Smith and Frankie Wainman used. John was helping to close the gap between the top drivers and himself by matching them in terms of equipment.

Perhaps the narrowing of the gap was best illustrated at the championship meetings, the big events that drew all the best drivers. His position as one of the top drivers in the grading list meant that John was invited to race in the British Championship for the first time in 1978 - he would also have qualified in 1977 but there was no championship meeting that year. Each driver raced in three of eight heats, starting once from the front third of the grid, once in the middle third, and once from the rear. Results from the heats were then collated to form a grid for the British Championship final. John finished all of his heats, each time making a small improvement: first ninth, then eighth, then seventh. Dave Mellor won the final in a shock result – it was his first ever final victory – and John steered his car home in sixth.

Two weeks after the British Championship drivers gathered for the inaugural European Championship, a weekend-long event held at Long Eaton on Saturday and Rochdale on Sunday. A normal meeting with heats, consolation, final and Grand National took place on both days, but one of the heats on each day was designated the European Championship race and had the best drivers in it. Results from the two races were then collated and a champion crowned. John had a respectable position in the final rankings with finishes of fourth and seventh. The new European Champion, Stuart Smith, only claimed his title after a two-car race-off against Mike Close. Close had won the first European Championship race with Smith fifth, the positions were reversed the following day. Both men dominated the weekend; Smith won the meeting final at Long Eaton while Close won the Rochdale final.

For John it was two decent performances in his first two major championships, and he followed them up by qualifying for the World Final. He started from the seventh row of the World Semi-Final for the second year in a row, courtesy of three final finishes in four qualifying events. This time John managed to get through the majority of the pack and steered his car home in sixth, enough to earn him a place on the grid in the World Final at Belle Vue, again on the seventh row of the grid. The five cars that came home in front of him in the World Semi-Final started in front of him, together with the first five cars from the other semi-final. Two foreign entrants, Dutchmen Rien Rutjens and Lambert Keulen, were designated the third row.

Stuart Smith was hot favourite to win the race from pole, defending champion Mike Close was on the outside of the second row. A number of younger drivers were also in the mix and made up the rest of the first three rows: Glyn Pursey had raced for two years longer than John, new British Champion Dave Mellor only started racing at the end of 1975, while Bert Finnikin and Dave Berresford were still relatively young.

Once again, it was not to be Smith's year. He failed to finish the first lap; Pursey despatched him into the steel fence wires on the first turn. Mellor continued his dream year and snatched the victory; John Hillam finished second and Pursey was third. The cars continued past the chequered flag: Brian Powles, Finnikin, Close, John Aldridge. Then, in eighth place, was John, his first finish in a World Final.

It was a commendable achievement, but a single race alone proved nothing. After all, John Aldridge finished in front of John, a driver who would go through his career with only six race victories and no victories in meeting finals. But John had also performed well in other championships, qualified for nearly every final in the meetings that he attended, and consistently finished those. John now had to be considered a contender, albeit an out-side one, for major trophies. The new wearer of the gold roof, Dave Mellor, had only won two meeting finals in his career when he won the World Championship. John had also won two meeting finals by the end of 1978.

Another major event occurred in John's life in 1978, but this time outside of stock cars. He married Liz, and the start of the racing season saw John setting up home as well as tinkering with his car. Liz realised that stock cars would play a major part in their domestic life, especially since the couple met through the sport. Liz's brother, Harvey Lodge, was a driver from Mirfield in West Yorkshire who made his debut at Rochdale in October 1976, the same meeting in which John claimed his first final win. Liz attended many meetings with Harvey, and was soon dating John. Within fifteen months they were married and she was migrating across the Pennines to make her home in Lancashire.

The 1979 season dawned brightly. John turned out on track in a car sporting a coat of white paint instead of the brushed-aluminium silver he had used so far. His new look helped him to a third career final victory in his third meeting of the season. Just like the previous two, the final win came at Rochdale, a circuit that saw most of John's best performances in the early years. This one was particularly fine. John came out and took the chequered flag in heat 1 from Frankie Wainman and Eric Hullah, then repeated the win in the final. The quality of opposition in the final was outstanding: of the eight other finishers six wore red tops, and the second placed driver, Allan Barker, was about to begin a phenomenal period that saw him win ten finals and shoot up the grading list to first place, finishing the season as a superstar.

Rochdale was certainly John's favoured track, and the second meeting of the season there saw John win both his heat and Grand

National. As the season progressed, however, he was disappointed that he failed to finish in any other finals there, although he won two other heats. John's other local track, Nelson, was on its final lap. After twelve years of hosting stock car meetings, the stadium at which John first watched the sport was compulsorily purchased and demolished to make way for the new M65 motorway. John recorded his seventh race win in the first heat at the track's last meeting. The farewell final was won by John Hillam, his only meeting final win at Nelson despite racing there for a decade. As it happened, the path of the motorway was diverted at the last moment and ran past the site of the old stadium, but by then it was too late and stock cars had moved on.

Mike Parker already had a local replacement. Blackburn had been hosting stock car races since 1978, although the Thursday evening meetings did not fit around John's work commitments and he raced there only twice in each of the first two seasons. Only once Nelson was gone and racing was scheduled on Saturdays did John become a regular at Blackburn. On his infrequent appearances John found that the short tarmac track was a similar venue to White City, requiring excellent traction and cornering, but whereas White City was almost circular and drivers were rarely able to fully open the throttle, Blackburn had straights that allowed drivers to get up more speed.

Having made satisfactory debuts in the major championships in 1978, John hoped to follow Dave Mellor's example and win a title early in his career. However that would have to wait for at least another year as John's championship form was disappointing in 1979. First up was the season-long Grand Prix Series. Designed to celebrate the silver jubilee, 25 years since stock car racing was introduced to the UK, the competition was given a big boost when the Daily Mirror offered generous sponsorship and prize money. That brought many of the best drivers to the Grand Prix

Series meetings looking to claim a share of the pot. They competed in a fourteen-round competition in which points scored were accumulated in a league table. At every round each driver raced in two out of five heats, the positions of which made up the grid in the final. Unlike many of his fellow competitors, John did not make the long journey south to Harringay in north London for the opening round, nor did he choose to travel to Northampton, Leicester and Hartlepool. Of the ten rounds that John did race, he only made it into the top ten in the final at White City, Blackburn and Nelson.

Perhaps a one-off meeting like the British Championship at Belle Vue would be a more realistic prospect for success. John Lund did win heat 7, but it was actually the 'other' John Lund from Gisburn. Having helped the original John in the pits during 1976 and 1977, the other John decided that he wanted to be out on track himself. He made his debut in 1978 driving a self-built car under the number 95, and during his first season won the Novice of the Year title, giving him bragging rights over his namesake – he won a title that the most successful stock car driver failed to win! The British Championship heat that John Lund 95 won was one of the few times he outperformed John Lund 53, who finished seventh in the same race. Neither driver finished their other two heats in the top ten, nor finished the final that Mike Close won.

The European Championship was held at Harringay, so John did not attend. By now well adrift in the Grand Prix Series, that left only the World Championship to aim for. John was allocated the World Semi-Final at Sheffield and started from the sixth row of the grid, marginally better than his seventh row start of the previous two years by virtue of finishing one place higher in the qualifying rankings. It made no difference, however, as John failed to finish. This year, he would watch Frankie Wainman win his solitary World Final as a spectator.

Of course, the possibility of a major championship was there, but nobody, least of all John himself, expected him to win. After all, he was still only an occasional race winner; by the end of 1979 he had won 33 races and three meeting finals. The final grading list of 1979 compiled all the points scored during the season and ranked John eighteenth, hovering just two spaces ahead of demotion to blue top, three places lower than the previous year. Andy Stott, John's main rival during his first few years in the sport, had risen as far as seventh, only one place from being classified as a superstar. Stott had also won the prestigious World Long Track Championship in Holland in 1979. John was in danger of losing touch with his early-career rival.

Working long hours on the farm and travelling long distances to race stock cars put strain on John's family life. After a short, difficult period, John separated from Liz and they were divorced. John was still only 25 years old, and the anxiety caused by the separation explains why John's mind was not always fully focused on the track in the late seventies. He would learn from the painful experience, however, and the problems resulting from the early failure of his marriage helped to instil in John a passionate belief in the importance of family.

John threw himself into racing in an attempt to escape his domestic problems. During the winter of 1979 and 1980 John bought another big-block Chevrolet engine. He then built a new car to house it in, constructed on the standard square-cab model that had served him for the past two seasons. John and his new car slogged it out at race meetings, winning occasional heats or consolations: two each at White City, Rochdale, Blackburn and Sheffield, and a single win at Belle Vue. When John qualified for the final, which he did at most meetings, he had a good record of finishing in the top eight; although at the Grand Prix Series meetings John struggled again, this time only finishing in the final at two of the rounds.

In the World Championship qualifying rounds John performed steadily but not spectacularly, the high point being second place in the final at the last qualifying meeting at Long Eaton. Yet it was still enough to push John into fifth place in the standings and a place on the inside of the second row of the World Semi-Final at Bradford. It may have been intimidating starting at the front of the grid surrounded by superstars; Dave Hodgson, Stuart Smith, Brian Powles and Willie Harrison, but John did not let it show.

Hodgson and Smith roared away from the rest of the field when the green flag was waved, while Glyn Pursey, who started alongside John on row 2, found a better line through the first turn to take third place. The first three broke clear, and Pursey continued to progress by overtaking first Smith and then Hodgson, leaving the latter stranded in a bunch of parked cars at end of the far straight. That promoted John to third, but he was coming under determined pressure from Powles, who sneaked past. John retook third place, but Powles got in front once more. John then fell behind slightly, only to benefit when Powles fell victim to a flat tyre. John was back in third place, this time with a clear space behind.

Pursey led through to victory, Smith settled for second, John was very happy with third. It was an indication to John of how important it was to get a good grid position at the main championship events. Starting from the front, John was safe from the unpredictable shunts and crashes that inevitably happened in the middle of the pack at the start of the race. While those behind clawed their way out from the mass, the cars at the front were able to break free.

John now had a nervous month to wait. He would start the World Final from an excellent position on the third row. He had the British Championship to handle first, held at Hartlepool the weekend before the World Final. Two finishes in his three heats, in third and sixth, gave John a grid position of sixteenth for the final. That did not bode well for a great race. It went wrong almost straight away when John was trapped in a first-lap pile-up with Alex McDade and Sam Ostle, but when flames licked the underside of Ostle's car the starter quickly waved his red flag and signalled a restart. John's car was undamaged, so he had a reprieve and a second chance. This time he got away safely. Through a combination of luck and skill John manoeuvred his way through the field. He made steady progress as big guns like Stuart Smith and Frankie Wainman were forced out of the race, but there was just too much to do, and John finished the race in fifth. It was another illustration of the importance of a good grid position in major championship races. John was too far back at the start to trouble the front-runners, while Glyn Pursey had a relatively easy drive to the title.

Having won both the Bradford World Semi-Final and a toss of the coin with the other semi-final winner, Pursey had the privilege of starting the World Final at Coventry from pole position. As the current British Champion and European Champion, Pursey must have been confident. John was less so. He was on the inside of row 3, with former World Champion Dave Mellor in between him and Pursey; two more former World Champions, Mike Close and Stuart Smith, lined up on the outside of the first two rows. Veteran driver Rod Falding started alongside John on row 3; Dutch superstar Rien Rutjens parked up behind John on row 4. Confined by great drivers on every side, John knew that he had to break free. If any one of the men alongside him got a few car lengths in front, John knew that he would struggle to reel them back in. He would have to make his move immediately.

The cars crept around the rolling lap in grid order, gradually increasing their speed as they rounded the final turn. As the green flag fell each driver slammed their foot to the floor and their engines roared. Accelerating down the home straight, the cars slid on the shale surface as their tyres looked for traction. John edged into the middle of the track, while Stuart Smith did the same from the outside of the row in front. As the front of the pack slowed for the first turn, John did not. He shunted Smith hard, directly into the fence. John slowed enough to make the turn, but many did not, Mellor and Close among them. Chaos ensued as cars fought to get round the swiftly accumulating blockage, and the starter quickly decided that a restart was necessary. Red flags were waved, and the race was stopped.

Clearing the track took time, during which Smith was quickly out of his car to survey the damage. He had a cracked radiator, normally the kind of wound that would end a race, but this was the World Final. Smith had time to fix the radiator and make it back to his place on the grid in the half hour delay as the marshals made everything ready for the restart.

When the restart came, John saw no need to alter his tactics. This time, however, he was not able to repeat the big hit. The front-runners made it round the first turn without any mishaps and John remained in fifth. Smith broke out from the chasing pack to take the lead, followed by Mellor, Close, Pursey and John. John forced his way past Pursey for fourth, and was handed his next position at three-quarter distance when Close retired onto the centre green. That left John in third, and as each of the top four drivers opened up a bit of a gap between themselves and the car behind, the race became a procession for the last few laps.

Smith became World Champion for the third time and savoured a title that had been a long time in coming. Dave Mellor finished second; John had achieved an excellent third place. It was his first time on the podium in a major event and his name would go down on the roll of honour in future World Final programmes.

That was not enough for John. He did not want to be remembered merely as a footnote in stock car history, a driver who once gained a third place in a World Final. John's aim was simple: he wanted to climb two steps and stand on top of the podium.

Two cars and an aerofoil - new tricks in the hunt for success

4

Superstar
1981-1985

In his quest for a major championship win, John decided to keep doing as he had done for the first five seasons of his career: get his car set up as well as possible and go out to win every race he could. There was little doubt that Stuart Smith, Frankie Wainman, Mike Close and Brian Powles were drivers with more experience and better cars, but luck always plays a key role in full-contact motorsport and John needed only one slice of good fortune to make a breakthrough.

April 1981 saw John take three race wins: two heats at Blackburn and a consolation at White City. It was a good start to the season, but things got even better in May. Having failed to finish his first heat at a soggy Grand Prix Series meeting at Rochdale, John won heat 5 to claim a decent grid position in the final. He then passed the chequered flag first in the final, helped by Frankie Wainman crashing on lap 2, Stuart Smith retiring on lap 4 and long-time leader John Hillam having engine trouble towards the end. It was John's first meeting final victory for over two years. He did not have to wait so long for his next one, which came two weeks later at the next Rochdale meeting, where John won heat and final again. In heat 3 he showed good, controlled use of the bumper, shoving local rival Len Wolfenden wide to overtake him and repeating the manoeuvre on Stuart Smith. In the final, Wolfenden finished just behind. John had now won five career finals, all at Rochdale.

Only five days later there was a sixth, and this time John broke his duck at other tracks. Having finished third in his heat at White City, John lined up for the final against a strong grid including Stuart Smith, Frankie Wainman, Mike Close, Dave Hodgson, Doug Cronshaw, Dave Berresford and Len Wolfenden. On wet, greasy tarmac, John managed to get to the front of the pack with Close just behind him. Hodgson and Smith were also fast, but John and Close had enough speed themselves to maintain enough of a gap between them and the battle for third. Hanging on in front of Close until the end, John was ecstatic to claim his first meeting win on tarmac.

The following day a confident John travelled to Long Eaton for the British Championship. Consistent finishes in the heats in fifth, sixth and second place gave him a grid position on the third row for the championship race. Nigel Whorton and Rod Falding made up the front row, with Brian Powles and Stuart Smith behind. John sat alongside Willie Harrison on row 3.

A poor start by Falding relegated him down the order, while Powles clipped the fence on the opening lap causing his own retirement. As the cars passed the starter at the end of the first lap, Whorton led from Smith in second and John in third. After four laps Whorton left a small gap on the inside through which Smith dived through for the lead. Another four laps passed and Whorton made the same mistake, allowing John to sneak through for second. Smith had opened up too much of a lead for John to make up and he drove to a safe victory, but John pulled clear of Whorton, who acted as a barrier against the other cars vying for a podium finish. It was a great result. Having finished third in the World Final the previous season, John had risen to second at the next major championship.

With a consolation win at Blackburn and heat wins at Belle Vue and Bradford, John pushed his way up the grading list. Ranked seventh in the red tops at the start of May, by the end he was second and knocking on the door of the superstars. John's attitude was to take each race and meeting at a time rather than looking at the grading list, but others were beginning to notice that he was close to becoming one of the sport's highest-ranked drivers for the first time.

Although June did not match up to the heady heights of May, John did enough, including three race wins and a number of podiums, to push his way through the grade ceiling and become a superstar. He still raced under a red roof but could now display flashing amber lights as well. He would start at the back of the red tops alongside the other superstars: Stuart Smith, Len Wolfenden, Frankie Wainman, Mike Close and Dave Berresford.

Stuart Smith was still the man to beat and had been given the honour of racing under number 1. As well as wearing the gold roof, Smith was about to win his thirteenth consecutive National Points Championship, awarded to the driver who scored the most grading points during the season. Smith's combination of racing genius and his dedication to turn up at as many meetings as possible throughout the season meant that the second-placed driver in the grading list was often some distance from him.

Smith's skill and race craft was far beyond that of his opponents, and John was among his many victims. In one Bradford meeting John followed Smith round the track, rubbing his front bumper against the back of Smith's car, waiting for the perfect moment to pounce. Smith saw that a car had parked up against the wall halfway along the home straight and aimed right for it. John followed behind, concentrating only on his rival in front. At the last moment Smith twitched his car to the left, just missing the stranded car. John was oblivious to the danger until it was too late and ploughed into the back of it. Smith continued on to an easy win; John was out of the race.

Yet it could easily swing the other way too. At White City on 11th July the stars and superstars scythed through the field, by the sixth lap John was in the lead followed by six other red tops. Smith pushed past John on lap 9 and stayed there for the next ten laps and it seemed like he would take another comfortable win. John had yet to give up, however, and launched Smith into the fence with such force that his car was wedged there. It was a brave manoeuvre that deserved to win the race, but a flat tyre forced John out almost within sight of the chequered flag and handed an unexpected victory to Len Wolfenden.

Jousting with Smith was part of John's continuing stock car education. At the start of his career John had a reputation of being a little wild and over-eager to use his bumper. Although he wasn't overly aggressive, he found that he was trying to go faster than his car was capable of. Sometimes he got away with it but often he did not, and the resulting crashes were expensive in terms of time and money. At the start of the 1980s, John made a conscious decision to ease back a little and keep out of trouble.

John's strong showing during the early part of the 1981 season earned him a place on the inside of the second row of the grid for the World Semi-Final at Northampton, although he would have preferred the chance to race in the second semi-final at Rochdale. Perhaps the unfamiliar track caused John to start poorly. Not only did he allow front rowers Glyn Pursey and Stuart Smith to get away on the first lap, but Frankie Wainman, Doug Cronshaw and Bert Finnikin also passed him from the outside rows. John hung on in sixth place, the last of a small group that made the early running and broke free of the chasing pack. By halfway round John was trading places with Wainman and Pursey for fourth, fifth and sixth, while Smith, Cronshaw and Finnikin fought over first, second and third. Smith was dumped out of the race with five laps to go when he lost grip on a patch of oil and slammed into the fence, but the others all avoided it and passed the chequered flag: first Cronshaw, then Finnikin, Pursey, Wainman and John. Although he finished at the back of the front runners, John made certain that he would have a chance at the World Final.

After holding superstar status for two months, John was leap-frogged by Glyn Pursey and went to the World Championship at Bradford back in star grade. He took up the outside berth on row 6 of the World Final grid. Although it was a dangerous spot, squeezed in the middle of the pack, it was a place from which a run to the gold roof could still be mounted.

The first lap saw all the cars away safely. John was still in the race, but stuck in the pack and with plenty still to do if he was to dispute the lead. Within a lap or two any possibility of John or anybody else getting close enough to challenge faded. Len Wolfenden, helped by a water-injected engine, powered away from pole and stayed there until the finish. It was one of the easiest World Final wins and quite a few drivers peered under Wolfenden's bonnet in the pits to see how he had his set up his car so well for the big race. Nevertheless, there were other positions to fight for. Brian Powles started alongside John on the sixth row and steered his way through to finish in second. John also made good progress through the pack but was unable to pass Mike Close and Frankie Wainman, and finished in fifth. A gap then separated John from sixth-place Rien Rutjens.

John finished 1981 in a positive fashion, with strong aggressive driving which saw him win nine more races. Two came at Blackburn, heat and Grand National, in a meeting where he also finished third in the final. He briefly led that race too, but a misjudged line through a turn gave Frankie Wainman and Stuart Smith an open invitation to pass. Two of the race wins were meeting finals, one at a wet White City on 19th September, his last victory there before the track closed at the end of the season, and one at Hartlepool on 27th September, another tarmac track. He also gave away a certain second place in an Aycliffe final by sliding wide on the final turn to pass an abandoned car, leaving the shorter, quicker inside line to a grateful Stuart Smith.

A strong September was followed by a quiet October. John loaned his car to his old friend and mechanic George Braithwaite, who had raced in five meetings over the past two seasons and now added another four in mid-October. Three race wins, including heat and meeting final at White City, were signs that Braithwaite had potential beyond the pits. John made only four October appearances, two each on the first and last weekends of the month. Among those meetings John planted Willie Harrison in the fence to take first place in an Aycliffe final but lost the lead with three laps to go to Mike Close. John added to his second place in the meeting final with a heat and Grand National win, collecting a healthy total of points and prize money, although his absences meant that he would not start off as a superstar in 1982. He was, however, hard on the heels of the drivers above him in the grading list, ready to take advantage of any slip-ups.

*

1982 was a season of change. Stuart Smith relinquished his hold on the National Points Championship, having had an iron grip on it for over a decade. Business commitments meant that he stepped back from regular racing, choosing to concentrate on the big championship meetings only. Dave Hodgson retired from racing after he suffered a serious neck injury at Hartlepool. Brian Powles, who took second place in the World Final and European Championships, also decided to quit racing. His surprise retirement was blamed on a lack of money and the cost of racing. Although Powles returned after a year, it was never with the same commitment and he won only a single race three years after the comeback.

Money was also the catalyst for Len Wolfenden's wrangles with the stock car authorities. The World and European Champion expected greater reward for his success, especially what he thought was a measly prize of £1150 for winning the World Final, and led a campaign for greater prize money and better appearance money for the top drivers. It was certainly getting more expensive to race. One of the biggest drains on cash supplies were tyres, the price of which seemed to be endlessly rising. Wolfenden's crusade alienated many and threatened a schism in the stock car world, but one driver who stayed clear of the political squabbling was John. Although he might display plenty of aggression on the track, off it he was non-confrontational and wanted to avoid the strife and bickering.

A busy farmer, John did not have the time to dedicate to the numerous committee meetings and behind-the-scenes manoeuvres that went with a political role in the sport. As his father slowly passed over the reigns of the farm, John stepped up his involvement. He was lucky that his father was always flexible and willing to work the unpopular evening and weekend shifts, staying behind to milk and feed the cows while John went to race.

In return John put in the early shifts, often being the first in the cow sheds.

The farm was slowly expanding. From an initial base of 150 acres, Norman and John added to the acreage with new purchases and rentals. The land that made up the farm grew to about 230 acres, and they took on a further 140 acres in various pockets dotted around the local area, totalling enough land to support 250 cows. The growth was necessary if the dairy farm was to survive. Supermarkets were rapidly taking over the shopping needs of people throughout the country and small farms could not compete with their substantial buying power which squeezed profit margins ever tighter. The farm machinery and equipment were a fixed overhead cost, so John needed more land and cows to make a profit.

John's farming wage helped with his expensive motorsport habit. All his racing was self-funded, there were no gifts bestowed upon him by his parents. Although they supported their son, they thought he was crackers spending a lot of time building a car and then wrecking it every weekend. John's savings were invested in his stock car and he could not afford luxuries like a road car.

It meant that he had to look after the pennies. When John decided that he needed a new engine in his car, he sought an old one that seemed to fit his requirements. It was another big block Chevrolet and one with quite a history. As far back as 1976, John's first season in the sport, the engine drove Stuart Bamforth to victory in the World Final. It passed to Richie Ahern, then Neil Brigg, under whose stewardship the engine exploded. Although it looked terminal, John bought the engine and spent time in the workshop getting it running again.

A second reason why John was too busy to get involved in the politics of the sport was his relationship with a new woman. His new girlfriend, Sarah, lived locally but had never crossed paths with John. That changed when she travelled home from work to be confronted with a herd of cows crossing the road. John gave her a cheerful wave of thanks when the cows had crossed and Sarah went on her way. The timing of her journey seemed to coincide with John's farm duties, and Sarah kept finding her route home blocked. John and Sarah started chatting, and the relationship developed from there. Soon she would become the new Mrs Lund.

John kept his head below the parapet and out of the political arguments, but he certainly benefited from the ructions of early 1982. Since Hodgson, Smith and Powles dropped out of the race for grading points there were a few gaps at the top of the table, allowing John to climb back to superstar grading, where he stayed all year. John also committed to racing more often. Crewe was a welcome addition to the racing schedule, a relatively close track with a wide shale oval that offered plenty of opportunity for fast, sideways driving. Tracks like Long Eaton and Coventry began to be regular additions to the Lund itinerary rather than occasional sojourns. As long as he could do his work first and get there, John was happy to race. At Sheffield on Mondays and Bradford on Fridays, John could do a full day of work and still be there in time for the first heat. The meetings all added up, and by the end of the season John had racked up 91 race meetings, behind only Frankie Wainman in terms of appearances.

Where Stuart Smith appeared, he was still the one to watch. Where he was not, there were three key men to beat. The first two were track specialists: Mike Close dominated at Aycliffe and Blackburn, while Bert Finnikin prevailed at Northampton and Bradford. Finnikin came from a stock car family, the son of Charlie and brother of Alan. Bert started racing in 1973 and rose to prominence in 1977 with a host of final wins that kept him a star or superstar for the next few years, and only geography (he was based in Leek, and struggled to attend some meetings) meant that he was not a superstar more often. The third challenger was Frankie Wainman, whose consistency meant that he was also a man to be watched, and he performed particularly well at Rochdale. Wainman built up a strong lead in the National Points Championship, but his form began to fall away mid-way through the season. Close gradually pulled him in, overtaking him in October and holding the lead in the final grading list to take the National Points Championship. John, mainly by virtue of his high number of appearances during the season, took third place in the championship. He was some 350 points behind Wainman and only twenty ahead of Finnikin, who had raced in 22 fewer meetings. Indeed, John actually had the lowest points-per-meeting average of the top eleven drivers. His third place was a reward for consistency rather than spectacular performances.

Perhaps frustrated by his lack of success – in the first half of the season John won only one meeting final, at Blackburn on 10th April – John began to drive more aggressively on track. It all seemed to begin at Hartlepool on 18th July. Having won his heat, John looked for a double by winning the meeting final too. His opponents took each other out with heavy hits and John initially stayed clear of trouble, nipping through the inside as others slid wide. He overtook Andy Stott to take the lead, having already been the beneficiary when Stott whacked Colin Gautry and John Toulson. It was true stock car racing, fierce action all over the track, but John seemed oblivious to the brutality around him. Until, that is, Stott retook the lead by nudging John wide. John reacted with a massive clobber into Stott's back bumper and the two flew into the fence, scraping along it, taking Frankie Wainman with them. John recovered to finish the final five laps and complete the race, but not before five other cars had passed him.

It was almost as if the carnage in the Hartlepool final reawakened John's old aggressive side. The next weekend at Rochdale, yellow-top Ray Leigh, a sparring partner from as far back as 1976, reopened a dormant feud. Leigh was leading the meeting final when John, who was a lap down, nudged his back bumper and caused him to spin. Leigh kept his engine running and rejoined the race, only to be put into the fence by John on his next circuit of the track. Leigh was fuming by what he considered to be John's unsporting racing and tried to force John into the fence in the Grand National just as waved yellow flags were bringing racing to a temporary halt. John retaliated by shoving Leigh into the fence instead. The feud looked set to continue through the race as Leigh reversed out of the fence and set off in pursuit of John, but Leigh got stuck on the high kerb on the inside of the track. The ill-feeling simmered until Bradford, three weeks later. Leigh tried to get recompense by waiting for John to pass him before launching himself in a big hit, aiming to stick John into the fence. He missed and smacked Ian Smith instead. Smith, an innocent bystander, was forced out of the rest of the meeting with the damage his car suffered, while Leigh seethed on.

By the Aycliffe meeting on 5th September, John was still dishing out hits with his front bumper. In the first heat, blue-top Eric Hullah was peeved when John shoved him into Pete Morton, and tried to spin John out with three laps to go even though John was a lap ahead. Again John escaped; Hullah did not manage to pull off his bold manoeuvre. John went on to an easy third place behind Stott and Wainman.

A rejuvenated, aggressive driving style may have been enough to deal with lower-grade drivers, but it was not enough to save John from mediocrity at the major championships. John finished seventh in the European Championship, but did slightly better at the British Championship. Finishes of fifth, fourth and sixth in the heats gave John a good grid position on row 5 for the championship race, in which he came home in fifth.

Having started the World Semi-Final at Leicester, an unfamiliar track, from fifth, John was slightly disappointed to finish in ninth. Willie Harrison, Dave Berresford and Glyn Pursey were away and safe in the first three positions, but John was fighting for fourth with Stuart Smith, Frankie Wainman and John Toulson. Leaving his rear end exposed at the exit of one turn was enough for Wainman to spin John, leaving him facing the wrong way as five or six cars got through. John recovered and got facing the correct way again, but without enough time to recover the lost places. That gave him a grid position on the eleventh row for the World Final at Belle Vue, a track where John was much happier to race. However, by the end of the World Final he was on the centre green. He watched Harrison hold off Close to take his only World Championship in 28 years of racing. Harrison was a popular winner, having been involved in the sport since its earliest days, and his example proved that John, a relative novice with a six-year career under his belt, still had plenty of time left to prove himself at the highest level.

A trio of final wins in nine days in September, at Sheffield, Hartlepool and Blackburn, was the high point of the countless miles travelled on English roads during the 1982 season. The Sheffield victory came in fortuitous circumstances. Creeping into the final with eighth place in the fourth heat, John watched his opponents drop like flies in the final, and he finished the race with half a lap advantage over Mike Close and the other four finishers. Having waited a long time for a meeting final victory, the next came within a week. The Hartlepool win, also in front of Close, was a better performance on a level playing field. A second lap pile-up disposed of most of the yellow and blue tops, but all of the red tops remained. John pushed his way past John Toulson and Andy Stott for the lead and used backmarkers as barriers to prevent Stott and Close getting near his back bumper. Just like Sheffield, John ran home a comfortable victor. Three days later, John made a rare midweek appearance at Blackburn. Stott and Frankie Wainman were early leaders in the meeting final, but both were forced out with flat tyres. It was still not easy for John, however, since he had been pushed wide early in the race and had to pass Len Wolfenden, Close, Toulson and John Dowson before the chequered flag.

John's strong run to the end of the season continued with a second consecutive Hartlepool final win where he clearly had the fastest car on track. A last meeting final victory came in John's last appearance of the season. On the drying Long Eaton shale, John judged the conditions best to take wins in both heat and final. That made five meeting final victories in three months. Although John may have been a little unhappy with his performances in the first half of the season and in the major championships, he had successfully turned his season round with a renewed, attacking style and ended the second half on a high.

The money problems that began to rear their head in 1982 escalated over the winter. For a while the pessimists in the sport declared that stock car racing was doomed, floundering as penny-pinching promoters were held hostage by greedy drivers. A power struggle in the British Stock Car Drivers Association saw a faction led by Len Wolfenden demand modernisation and a better deal for drivers. Their key demands were better payment for drivers, fewer fixtures and a shorter season, each designed to make stock car racing more profitable for the top drivers and more viable for lower-grade drivers. Yet despite the worries of the doom-mongers and the protestations of both sides, stock car racing was actually in good shape. It had the best publicity of all when ITV screened certain stock car meetings on World of Sport, and the sport was getting good coverage in the Daily Mirror as a direct result of their sponsorship of the Grand Prix Series.

John also had a personal sponsor, Townson Tractor Exports, a Lancashire-based firm who first supported John in 1979. The money ex-driver Colin Townson gave John to display his business name on the side of the car helped to fund the construction of a new car for the 1983 season. New rules and regulations regarding roll cages, which now required six tubular posts, caused John to depart slightly from his usual design to which he had faithfully stuck for the last four or five cars. Rather than a square cab, John now built cabs with an angled back, giving it a more contemporary look. John's old square-cab car was retained as a spare and used by George Braithwaite, who started racing more regularly. Braithwaite won four races in March and April, enough to boost him straight from white top to star grade in the first grading list of the season.

Braithwaite was just one of a number of drivers who were racing Lund-built cars. Ian Smith and Dave Wadsworth were among John's buyers in the late seventies, and their positive reports meant that John's reputation as a reliable builder was growing. John was building a new car most winters and usually sold his older race cars to help fund the new ones. Profits gained from selling the cars and prize money accumulated at meetings were put back into improving his setup. It all contributed to John's organic growth and slow, steady improvement.

The new car helped John make a sustained challenge for the Grand Prix Series for the first time. The previous season it had been shortened to seven meetings, this time there were six. The new streamlined format allowed John to compete at all rounds, and he won the final at Coventry on 2nd July. Elsewhere in the series, John finished third in the final at Leicester and fifth at Sheffield. When the points were accumulated and counted at the end of the last meeting of the series, John was third. Dave Mellor won, snatching the lead at the last meeting; Willie Harrison slipped from the top spot he held from the first round. John's £250 prize money was a useful addition to the Lund Racing Team coffers.

The Coventry final win in the Grand Prix Series was John's first meeting final victory of the season. He had been forced to wait until 1st May for his first race win, in the Grand National at Aycliffe, although a number of second and third places showed that he came close in March and April. Nevertheless, podium finishes were not enough to stop John dropping back into star grade. He ranked fourth in the stars in the May grading list and gradually clawed his way back up the list, to third in June, second in August and top of the star drivers in September.

The grading lists neatly capture John's improvement over the season. Once he had broken his duck at Coventry, he followed up with a heat and final win at Blackburn seven days later. At the British Championship at Rochdale on 24th July, he started with a flyer and won heat 1 ahead of Mike Close and Frankie Wainman. Finishes of seventh and fourth in his other two heats gave John a decent grid position on the outside of the second row in the championship race. Len Wolfenden leapt away from pole position when the green flag fell, and only John seemed to have the speed on the uneven Rochdale shale to keep up with him. He tried to close the gap, but Wolfenden kept a safe distance between him and John, not allowing any opportunity for a desperate lunge. John seemed safe in second until a late charge brought Stuart Smith close to his back bumper and he knocked John into the fence to take second. John recovered, but only after Bert Finnikin had driven past for third place. John had to settle for fourth, just ahead of George Braithwaite.

Eight days later, John gave himself an excellent foundation to challenge for the World Championships. Three podiums in the finals of his seven qualifying meetings meant that John finished second in the qualifying lists and was given pole position in the second World Semi-Final at Sheffield. Leading from the first turn, John anxiously watched for a challenge from behind. Stuart Smith was his nearest rival at the start of the race, but John drove defensively and kept him at bay. Mike Close then passed Smith and caught John quickly. Rather than end up in the fence, John allowed Close through and settled for second. However, as the starter signalled the penultimate lap, John saw Close clip a stationary car on the far straight and his rear offside tyre rapidly deflated. John sneaked past with the finish line in sight to take the win, Smith still just off his back bumper in second. For the first time John would start a World Final from the front row. But first, just five days after his World Semi-Final win there was the small matter of a trip to Northampton, which was fast becoming the spiritual home of the European Championship. This time Mike Close did not suffer any last lap misfortunes and retained the title that he won the previous year. John trailed in a distant seventh after losing valuable ground on the first lap getting embroiled with Glyn Pursey and three blue tops.

The World Final was hosted by Coventry, the first time the race had returned there since John started on the third row in 1980 and despatched Stuart Smith into the fence to cause a restart. This time, John was in an even better position. Len Wolfenden won the other World Semi-Final at Hartlepool and won the toss of the coin which allowed him to start in pole position, with John on the outside of the front row. Smith and Bert Finnikin made up the second row, with Andy Stott and Mike Close on the third. Remembering his excellent performance three years before in which he finished third, John knew that he stood a real chance this time. If ever he would win the World Final, surely this would be it.

Wolfenden did not take full advantage of his luck in the coin toss and got the start wrong, allowing John to hit him wide and surge into the lead. Smith and Finnikin nipped passed Wolfenden for second and third. It was a great position for John to be in, but there was always the threat of Smith from behind. Seven laps in, when Mike Close became stranded across the track at the end of the home straight, Smith saw his chance. He nudged John, forcing him to take a wide line behind Close's car. That gave Smith the lead, but John managed to retain second place, slowly gaining on Smith who was being held up by a lap-down Wolfenden. A rollover by a Dutch entrant, Leon Cox, then brought out waved yellow flags and bunched the field back up.

This was John's chance. He knew that Smith would be vulnerable on the restart and determined to give him a whack from behind on the first corner. With his foot hovering over the accelerator, John waited for the green flag. Back down the track, Wolfenden decided to push Close's car off the track, and a well-meaning but foolish mechanic jumped into the Close car to steer it off the track.

The starter waved the green flag to restart the race, but his timing was abysmal. Wolfenden had not yet got Close's car off the track, and the green flags were waved when Smith, John and Finnikin were right underneath him on the home straight. Unable to see, the leaders had no idea that the race had restarted. The first driver with a decent view, Danny Clarke, dived down the outside and into the lead. Belatedly aware that racing had begun, drivers sheared across the track and caused chaos at the turn where the stranded Close car had now been joined by Wolfenden's. Smith leapt off in pursuit of Clarke but Finnikin and John collided, while further down the field Willie Harrison and Piet Keijzer locked together. Both Finnikin and John suffered punctures; Finnikin limped to the centre green, John tried to continue.

He managed only a few laps before he realised that it was useless and would wreck his chassis if he carried on racing, so he retired to the centre green alongside Finnikin.

Smith went on to catch and pass Clarke to win the World Championship, the first four-time winner. It was a final marred by a decisive incident of poor officiating. While Smith understandably celebrated his record-breaking achievement, a number of other drivers nursed their grievances. Chief among them was John, who was in the best position to benefit from the waved yellow flags. His cursing left those around him in no doubt as to his opinion of Mr Starter on this occasion.

At least the three major championships signalled a return to form. With a newly rebuilt and reconditioned Chevrolet engine in his car John won the meeting final at three consecutive meetings at Aycliffe; in August, September and October, and a heat and final at Hartlepool on 18th September. He also finished second to Bert Finnikin in the Grand National Championship, a race between the season's top points scorers in the end-of-meeting Grand National races. Initially Mike Close looked good for the win, but for the second time in a key race that season Close suffered a puncture on the penultimate lap and this time he slipped down all the way to eighth. John's improved results helped him get back among the superstars in the October grading list and he finished the season in sixth place. Bert Finnikin had stepped up his racing schedule and finished the year as National Points Champion, just ahead of defending champion Mike Close.

At the start of the 1983 season John dropped back into star grade after a relatively slow start to the year. He was careful to make sure this did not happen in 1984. A second car was added to the Lund armoury, allowing John to have separate tarmac and shale layouts. At this early stage there was little real difference between the two chassis, only in the suspension did John vary things. He tried using half elliptic springs but mounted in quarter elliptic fashion for tarmac, but that didn't work well. Once he cancelled that experiment, John shifted to a spring-over suspension for tarmac, and a spring-under suspension for shale.

Under the bonnet of the new car, which John elected to use for tarmac, was a big block Chevrolet engine formerly belonging to Brent Savage. Len Wolfenden was tasked with selling off Savage's equipment when he got in trouble with the law, and John voiced his interest in the engine and a transporter bus. The back seats of the bus had been removed, giving enough space for a stock car and spare parts, the front rows were left in place for John and his team.

Yet it was the engine in the shale car that performed best at the start of the season. John won the first race of the season, heat 1 in the opening meeting at Bradford, and followed it up with first place in the final and fourth in the Grand National. It was John's first meeting victory at Bradford and was followed up with another final victory at the second Bradford meeting of the season a month later. This time he also won the consolation and again finished fourth in the Grand National. John was showing excellent form at Bradford and he regretted that meetings would only be available for the first half of the season. In June Odsal Stadium was closed for refurbishment and to resurface the tarmac track with shale in preparation for the Speedway World Final the following year.

John's performances at Bradford, together with a final victory at Aycliffe, kept him secure in superstar grade. The British Championship at Belle Vue came the day after John's meeting win at Aycliffe, so he entered it with renewed confidence. He finished two of his heats, including one in second place behind Nigel

Whorton, qualifying safely for the final. There he drove a consistent race to edge his way through the field and finish in fifth.

Three days later the stock car bandwagon rolled into Bradford for what should have been a typical mid-season meeting, the last before it closed for refurbishment. John qualified for the final in second and finished in the same position in the final behind Mike Close. He also raced in the Grand National and finished fifth. Soon after the meeting, however, all thoughts of racing were overshadowed when news filtered through that Steve Froggatt, a yellow top driver who had been taken to hospital with concussion, suddenly deteriorated and died. It was the first fatality in the sport since Brian Wallace was killed in John's first season. John, like all the other drivers at the meeting, knew that Steve was injured but was not aware how badly. As always, the instinct of a sportsman kicked in. He got in the car and blocked out all other thoughts to get on with racing, for the good of the spectators as much as himself. It was a sad moment in Bradford's fine stock car history.

John finished a mediocre tenth at the European Championship where John Cayzer took his only major championship win. It was a race in which John was far from challenging for the lead, but it was not as disappointing as the World Semi-Final. John did not earn as many World Championship qualifying points as he would have liked, so rather than starting on the front row of the World Semi-Final, he was on the outside of the second row. A silver lining was that the race was at Rochdale. Yet despite having a good knowledge of the rough shale track, he crashed out and was left without a place on the World Final grid. The big race was won by Stuart Smith, his second in a row and fifth World Championship title.

John's last positive results of the season came around the same time as the World Final. The weekend before the World Championship meeting he gained three second places in three races at Rochdale; a determined drive that seemed to signal that John felt he had something to prove. He did it again the day after the World Final with a meeting win at Aycliffe on 16th September.

Although John had won only four meeting finals compared with seven the previous season, and 19 races in total compared with the previous season's 34, he actually finished the National Points Championship in second place, a personal best finish. Frankie Wainman was the runaway winner, deserving the title with the joint-highest average points scored each meeting – the other driver equalling him was Stuart Smith, who was concentrating only on the major championships and qualifying rounds. John finished a meagre one and a half points ahead of third-placed Dave Berresford, but could truly claim to deserve his place near the top of the grading list. Unlike 1982, when he finished third but with the eleventh-highest meeting average, this time he had the fourth highest. Other than Wainman and Smith, only Andy Stott had a higher one. Although he had not passed the chequered flag first in as many races as the previous season, John had ground out more podium and top ten finishes, and was more successful in seeing his car through the Grand National race at the end of each meeting.

John's second place in the National Points Championship concluded a season that saw the beginning of a shift in track locations. Blackburn, Rochdale and Leicester hosted their final stock car meetings during 1984, each making away for new building developments. John regretted the loss of his local tracks. With Rochdale and Blackburn joining Nelson in the stock car graveyard, he could no longer do an afternoon's milking, go and race and be back in Clitheroe before the chip shop closed! More importantly, it also meant that John, like other drivers, needed to travel further afield to make sure that they could race, spending more in petrol. However, the loss of tracks meant that meeting clashes, with drivers forced to choose which they would attend, became increasingly rare. In 1984 there were clashing meetings on twelve occasions, the 1985 fixture list saw just five, each time involving Northampton. With the exception of those dates, spectators could now expect the best drivers to attend most meetings.

Surprisingly, one of the Northampton clashes involved the European Championship. At that meeting, on a Saturday afternoon in mid-August, John finished outside the top ten in the main event but stayed on at Northampton to finish fourth in heat 2, ninth in the meeting final and ninth in the Grand National. He then loaded up his car and headed sixty miles north on the M1, along with many other drivers, to compete in an evening meeting at Long Eaton. There John raced another three times, getting sixth in heat 2, tenth in the final and sixth in the Grand National. That meant a total of seven races in one day, to be followed with a meeting at Aycliffe the next day and Sheffield on Monday evening. There may have been less choice of meetings in 1985, but the life of a stock car driver was no less busy.

John was a beneficiary of the unpredictable Yorkshire weather in the Sheffield final. The race initially developed into a two-car run-off between Stuart Smith and blue top Ray Tyldesley until the heavens opened and, within the space of a lap, track conditions changed from dry shale to ice rink. Smith and Tyldesley were too close together and inevitably came to grief on the suddenly slick surface, while John had more space around him and carefully guided his car round them to the chequered flag.

As well as the European Championship, Northampton also hosted the British Championship, at which John finished all three heats, but with his results going in the wrong direction: second, sixth and eighth. That was enough to qualify on the fifth row of the grid, but by the end of the first lap it was obvious that

John was out of the running. Des Chandler started on the outside of the front row but lost control on the first corner. Although Frankie Wainman and Mike Close got past, John did not, and clattered into Chandler; Harry Smith and Murray Harrison followed in from behind. It put all four out of the race, while the drivers who started on the inside of the track got through safely. Four of the first five finishers at the end of the race started on the inside rows.

John started the campaign for the World Championship well, winning the final of the first qualifying event at Skegness in March, but he fell down the qualifying rankings when he failed to make the final in seven of the other eight meetings. That gave him a spot on the third row in the Belle Vue World Semi-Final. It was experience that counted in this race, with Mike Close taking the win from pole, followed by Len Wolfenden who battled through from the seventh row. John finished a World Semi-Final on the centre green for the second year in a row, having sustained damage in a three-way collision with Wolfenden and Neil Pokorny. He was a spectator for the World Final once again.

The World Championship meeting was a frustrating one for John. While Stuart Smith celebrated his third consecutive World Final win, matching Dave Chisholm's achievement from the 1970s and becoming the self-styled but undisputed maestro of stock car racing, John failed to finish in his meeting heat, consolation and Grand National.

At least he had something to celebrate in September. A week after the World Final, Sarah gave birth to James, their first child. John already survived with minimal sleep; early mornings on the farm were coupled with late evenings working on his stock cars. Now he had the unsocial hours of baby feeding and nappy changing to add into the equation!

Other than the Skegness World Championship qualifier and the Sheffield meeting two days after the European Championship, John won only one other final, on 19th May at Aycliffe. For the second season in a row, his record of race wins showed a downturn. This time he had won only three finals and nine races. His consistent form elsewhere was not enough to put him in the top three of the National Points Championship and John finished in fifth place. He was still comfortably among the superstars, but there were nine other drivers with higher meeting averages.

It was a worrying trend. John had shown signs of a breakthrough between 1981 and 1983, winning over 30 races each season. Now he was languishing in single figures. Although he was consistently towards the top of the grading list, he was failing to make the last, most important breakthrough to be a championship winner. A vital ingredient was missing – but what was it?

Celebrating success with James

5

World Champion
1986-87

John's drop in form over the last couple of seasons led him to decide that a radical rethink was needed. It was a decade since John had built his first stock car and the fundamental design of his cars had not changed very much in those ten years. True, there were some modifications and improvements, most notably the new roll cage in 1983, but the basic structure remained the same. Now it was time for a change. For the 1986 season John built a new tarmac car, selling on his old one to Brian Butterfield.

The most obvious change was the addition of an aerofoil winged roof. Stuart Smith was one of the first to introduce these in 1980, claiming that the aerodynamic effect helped the car to retain traction and speed on corners. His opponents were initially unconvinced and only a few drivers tried their own efforts: Mike

Close was an early convert, while Frankie Wainman, John Hillam and a few others reshaped their cabs to be more aerodynamic. Things changed in 1984 and 1985 when a flood of aerofoil roofs appeared on track; John was one of the few drivers left on the grid who did not use one. He remained suspicious of how well they helped in cornering and was reluctant to spend money on what he considered a needless extra. But the downturn in his results over the previous two seasons, coupled with his decision to slightly alter his chassis structure, meant that a new aerofoil roof was added both to the new tarmac car and the older shale car.

Under the bonnet of the new tarmac car was a reconditioned engine. The old tarmac engine which previously belonged to Brent Savage was not part of the package that Butterfield bought, so John took it out and gave it a close inspection. Although it was a runner, it seemed to lack power on occasion. John took it to Mike Huddart, who owned a dynamometer, and discovered that there was a problem with the camshaft. Huddart fitted a new one and gave the engine a thorough going over. A few days later John had a fully-functioning, race worthy engine.

His new car was complete and ready to race, but John required a little time to perfect its setup. He spent a lot of time fiddling with the suspension and chassis, trying to make sure that the new car got maximum power onto the track while retaining traction. His new chassis allowed him to adjust the degree of axle lead and chassis wedge, meaning that he could manipulate the cornering ability of the car. John found that the new car turned far better after he pushed the right hand side of both axles forward by about one and a half inches. The signs were good right from the start. In his first race of the season, John rushed through the field for first place in his heat at Northampton. He had found a winning formula on tarmac almost immediately.

Race wins began to come more regularly after six weeks of tinkering. Starting with a Grand National win at Northampton on 20th April, John won seven races over the next four weeks. None of them were finals; the first of those arrived in mid-May when John won both heat and final at Aycliffe. For the last five laps of the final, John had gradually closed the half-lap gap between himself and long time leader Mike Close. On the penultimate bend, Close was slowed a little by Ray Tyldesley, allowing John to attack on the last turn. Both cars went into the home straight side by side, but John had enough momentum to creep into the lead, winning by half a car length.

The next weekend he travelled to Long Eaton, finishing second in his heat and winning the final, passing Bert Finnikin, Frankie Wainman and Nigel Whorton as they tangled together. The following day was Northampton, where John won both heat and final again. John had far more speed than any other car and passed many opponents as though they were stationary. He had won three consecutive finals and also gained two wins and a second place in the heats, a massive vindication of his decision to build a new car.

As the season progressed, John continued to improve and develop his setup. Aycliffe was a particularly good circuit and saw six final wins, including one in which John won both heat and final and came second in the Grand National, less than a quarter of a lap behind winner Frankie Wainman despite starting a lap behind.

John discovered that tyre preparation was important at all tracks, but especially so at Aycliffe. Stock cars used cross-ply tyres that were not in optimum racing condition when brand new. Even when they were fitted with the right combination of stagger, size and pressure there was a big difference in how different tyres performed. John found the best formula through a gradual process of experimentation and experience. He used them on shale first to feather up the tyres and wear them in so their grip improved when they were subsequently used on tarmac. On a dry tarmac track, an almost bald, slick tyre was best, giving the greatest surface contact. However, when the track was wet, bald tyres were useless. On occasions when the Aycliffe tarmac was damp – which was more often than not – John used tyres that retained some tread to move water from out beneath the rubber.

John often used different tyres on the four corners of his car on tarmac: an Avon Turbospeed on the inside front, a Dunlop RS5 on the outside front, a Dunlop Weathermaster on the inside rear, and an Alliance off-road tyre on the outside rear. He had an abundance of tyres to choose from since Nigel Hardy, who rarely raced on tarmac, sold his tyres to John after he had used them on shale. John kept his best resources in hand for the most valuable races by saving some of his prepared tyres for meeting finals.

Victory at a new track, Newtongrange, was due to similar careful tyre preparation. Located just south of Edinburgh, it gave Formula 1 drivers a first trip north of the Scottish border in nearly thirty years. The meeting was marketed as the Scottish Championship to draw drivers north, although only 24 made the long journey. John looked at the tarmac track and decided that the tight corners and long straights were comparable to those at Aycliffe. Selecting similar tyres to those he would race in the northeast, John went out in his heat and won it. Now knowing that his tyre choice on this track was correct, he took a deserved victory in the final.

Elsewhere in the fixture list, stock car racing was forced to take a back seat at Bradford as Odsal Stadium became the temporary home for Bradford City after the Valley Parade fire. Cleethorpes looked like it might take over from Bradford in hosting Friday night meetings, but it was pulled from the schedule after only three meetings.

At the European Championship, the first major meeting held on the tarmac of Skegness, the grid was randomly allocated by drawing drivers from a hat. John found himself towards the middle of the pack, a draw that could have been worse but could have been better. Bobby Burns took full advantage of his luck in the draw and took an early lead. By half distance he still held on, followed by Bert Finnikin, Dave Berresford, John and Friedhelm Welters. The Dutchman had charged through from the back and continued to make strides towards the front by passing John. With two laps to go, Finnikin snatched the lead from Burns. A little further back, Welters failed in a thrust to get by Berresford and slowed down enough for John to retake fourth place. It stayed that way at the end with John just missing out on the podium.

At the British Championship at Long Eaton John qualified on the third row of the final with sixth, fifth and second in his heats. Andy Shaw started on pole having driven to victory in all three of his heats, an amazing achievement for a driver who won only nineteen other races in his eight year career, but he could not stand the pressure in the final and was soon despatched. Nigel Whorton kept the lead from the front row, followed by Bobby Burns and Bert Finnikin. All three had started on the outside of the grid; the drivers on the inside, including John, were held up by Dave Berresford and Shaw coming together. Nevertheless, John led the pursuing group that included Frankie Wainman and Jon Lander. A rollover on the far straight by Harry Smith allowed the six cars to bunch back up again. John used the opportunity to get past Finnikin, while Burns retired with a seized wheel bearing. John was now one car away from victory, but Whorton used the traffic as a barrier and kept hold of the lead until the end of the race. John was on the second step on the podium, matching his performance at the British Championship in 1981.

Having come seventh in the World Championship qualifying rankings, John started the Hartlepool World Semi-Final from the outside of the second row on the grid. He hoped to get through and into the lead quickly, a position from which he could control the race. He never had a chance. The two men on the front row, Mike Close and Ray Tyldesley, ploughed into the fence on the first turn and collected Bobby Burns, John, Bert Finnikin and Richard Ainsworth. Burns rolled, Tyldesley wedged in the fence, Finnikin and John both suffered punctures. Dave Tapping and Rod Falding spun but managed to rejoin. After one lap the lead was held by John Wright, who started way back on row 5. For the third year in a row John had failed to qualify for the World Final, an experience he found more frustrating than getting to the final and not finishing in it. Instead he went to the World Championship at Coventry to take place in the normal race meeting only, feeling like a spare part when it came to the hype and build-up to the main event.

Yet John could still finish the season a World Champion. In the month between the World Semi-Final and the World Final John spent a weekend in Holland for the Long Track World Championship. Although the title did not hold the same status as the British-based short track World Final, it was still a competitive meeting. To Dutch drivers it was the highlight of the season, and the best British drivers had been invited to compete since 1977. They had enjoyed some success there too: Ian Ireland won in 1979, Andy Stott won in 1981, and British drivers had finished second seven times.

The Long Track Championship, as the name suggested, was held on a track with straights four times longer than British tracks.

It was a tarmac surface, and since John had enjoyed some success at British tarmac tracks with his new car he thought it would be worthwhile putting his name forward to the BSCDA as one of the potential British representatives. John was selected alongside some long track veterans and hoped to gain valuable experience.

The arrangements to get there fell neatly in place. At the start of the season one of John's acquaintances from the late seventies got in touch. Pete Hall had raced occasionally in Formula 1 but focused more on Formula 2. A sponsorship offer from Brendan Markey, a major stock car supporter with a history of sponsoring top-class drivers like Mike Close and Len Wolfenden, tempted him back to the big league properly in 1986. Hall wanted to use Markey's money to buy a Lund-style car which was built for him by Dave Seed. Hall also wanted John to store the car for him and take it to race meetings on a transporter behind John's van.

A few months later, when John was considering racing in Holland, Markey offered to arrange the ferry crossing because he had experience of transporting plant hire equipment abroad. Moreover, he offered John use of a spare transporter bus that he had. Markey had sponsored Joe Jopling in 1985, agreeing that he fund a new car and buy a bus from Brian Powles. They soon parted company; Jopling kept the car but Markey retained the bus and had it gathering dust on one of his sites. John readily agreed to take the aging bus from him and in exchange put Markey's name on the side of his car. It was the first move in a sponsorship arrangement that would last for more than two and a half decades. The bus would also remain with John for that long!

John travelled to Holland in his new transporter bus using the ferry tickets organised by Markey. The ferry docked in Calais in darkness and the bus, which still had all the windows in place, looked much like a normal passenger vehicle and was waved through by the French officials. Mike Close and one or two others travelled over in transporter buses with panelled-over windows, and unknown to John had been ordered to park up in front of the customs point for a thorough search.

A few hours later the bus reached the Belgian border. Bobby Burns was parked up on the side of the road, a few hundred metres from border control, but John only saw him at the last moment and passed without stopping. A gruff border guard asked for the paperwork they needed to cross into Belgium. John had no idea what was required, so got the thick folder of documents that Markey had given to him and handed it over. Lacking both Flemish and French language skills, John waited mutely. Once he paid 20 Francs the guard was happy to wave him through.

John arrived at the stadium in Baarlo well before his fellow countrymen. When they finally joined him John learned that they had all gone through the third degree at Calais and the border about their intentions and been asked to provide official paperwork that listed their entire inventory. The European officials were concerned that the drivers were going to sell some of their equipment and return without declaring it. Most had been stopped at Calais while John bypassed them; Bobby Burns got through but could not provide the necessary documents at the Belgian border and was not allowed to cross. As John's bus had sailed past him, Burns was getting ready to return on the ferry to England. John had remained happily oblivious to all the aggravation, sailing through the customs points and border on his bus that looked unaltered in the dark!

That first trip to Holland was more for enjoyment and experience than any serious thoughts that John might actually win the Long Track Championship, but he performed well. The racing was very different; the long straights required a change in the gearing and differently prepared tyres. Nevertheless, John quickly adapted to the new conditions.

Starting towards the back of the grid, John had to take evasive action when a couple of cars that started in front went into the first corner with too much speed and lost control. He emerged unscathed but still at the back of the field. He then rounded the track a few times, avoiding a Dutchman whose car was on fire and who took out a flagpole on the centre green in his haste to park his car near the fire extinguishers. Just before half distance John followed him onto the centre green, though avoiding the flagpoles, his car having had enough of the long straights. Although he did not finish the Long Track Championship, John had learned about the track and won the following race and the Jac Claes Trophy that went with it.

The Baarlo trip helped John put his disappointment about the short track World Championship aside and he finished the season on a high. He gained a hefty bonus at Belle Vue in September, picking up a £1000 cheque for winning a one-off 'who dares wins' race. It was a great drive. First John had to survive three laps with Mike Close rubbing his back bumper, defending as best he could, until Stuart Smith side-swiped Close into the fence on the penultimate lap. With such a big prize at stake, it was no surprise when Smith launched a risky last bend attack a few seconds later. He went into the turn with too much speed and clattered the fence, leaving John to recover his line and cruise away for the win. Smith, recognising a great defensive drive, applauded John on his victory lap. John also won both heat and final in the penultimate Sheffield meeting of the season, and repeated the feat at the final Aycliffe meeting of the season. The heat at that meeting had particular significance as it doubled-up as the Grand National Championship. John won the race, holding off Frankie Wainman in second and Peter Falding in third. Together with the Scottish Championship, it was his second title of the season. They were not major championships, but there was little doubt that John was becoming a front runner for those too.

John's new car had proved a real turning point. He won 54 races including thirteen finals during the season, both personal bests by some distance. Frankie Wainman held onto the National Points Championship for the third consecutive season, his consistency in attendance and scoring giving him the highest number of appearances and best meeting average. John was not far behind. He finished second in the grading list, entirely by credit. He had raced the second highest number of meetings (79 compared to Wainman's 82) and had the second best meeting average (30 compared to Wainman's 33). Wainman finished with 2667 grading points, John had 2400. Bobby Burns was a distant third with only 1597.

Having failed to retain the gold roof at the World Championship, Stuart Smith decided to call time on his racing career. The new World Champion, Peter Falding, was a young driver who wore a yellow top the last time a driver other than Smith won the World Final. Falding was one of a new generation of drivers challenging for success. Among the others were Bobby Burns, Bert Finnikin, Ray Tyldesley, Nigel Whorton and John Lund. They were all born a decade or more after Smith and had the youthful energy required to spend countless hours on track, en route to meetings or in the workshop. Each of the new generation now jockeyed to see who would be the one to take over the mantle of the greatest stock car driver of all.

Stuart Smith's retirement led to a hastily arranged testimonial meeting on 7th December at Belle Vue. This out-of-season meeting gave drivers a chance to race in a less frenzied atmosphere, where grading, championship and qualifying points were not on the line. John won a clockwise race, which required careful handling in cars set up to only turn on an anti-clockwise track. Then at the usual Christmas holiday meetings, John secured a victory in the final at Belle Vue on Boxing Day. Those wins at Belle Vue were to prove vital experience for later in the season.

In between the off-season outings, John was back in the workshop building a new shale car for the 1987 season. His new tarmac car had been a resounding success and John wanted to reproduce the same form on the loose. The key was the big block engine that Mike Huddart had reconditioned the previous winter, it seemed to have much more power available. John went back to Huddart during the winter of 1986/87 with a second engine, the old Stuart Bamforth World Final winner that had been in John's shale cars since the early eighties, and asked for a similar rebuild. A new chassis was constructed to house the engine and the process of tinkering to get the setup just right began.

The new season started steadily. John's first race victory came in only his second meeting, and he was pleased that it was on the Bradford shale, newly-restored to the fixture list now that Bradford City had returned to Valley Parade. Not only did John win his heat, he also won the Grand National and finished third in the meeting final. John's first meeting final victory of the season came at Aycliffe on 22nd March. A number of podiums and heat wins followed before another final victory, again at Aycliffe, on 26th April. The same trend followed in the next month; John got on the podium and won a few heats before he won a third consecutive meeting final at Aycliffe, on 17th May.

Aycliffe was to prove John's best track of the season again, although his run of meeting victories was broken at the next meeting, Aycliffe's most important of the year, the European Championship. A flat tyre cost John the chance to compete for the championship race. Ian Smith won the race from blue top, the rest of the field seemed stunned that the Aycliffe master was out.

Ray Tyldesley won the meeting final; John failed to finish again. It was back to form after that; John won the next three meeting finals. Doug Cronshaw and John Toulson shared the spoils in two of the last four meetings, with John winning the other two. Over the course of the season, John won eight out of eleven Aycliffe meetings.

The first three Aycliffe victories helped John rise to the top for the first time when the grading list was issued in June. The other contributing factor was a major milestone in John's career. He won the British Championship held at Skegness on 24th May, just before the grading period closed. Skegness was a tarmac track, and John's form on the Aycliffe tarmac gave him some confidence, although each track had its own different idiosyncrasies and required a slightly different driving style. The corners at Skegness were less tight than Aycliffe, so it was important to keep speed through the corner to maintain good lap times.

The grid for the British Championship race was decided by the results of eight heats. To have a decent chance in the final it was important for John to gain a grid position near the front through consistently good finishes in the three heats he was allocated. John started strongly, going out in the first race of the day and bringing his car home in second behind Joe Jopling. In heat 3, John went one better and took the chequered flag first. His place on pole position for the final was confirmed when he won heat 6.

Starting at the front of the grid on a racing surface that he had dominated for the past season and a half meant that John was the favourite to win. He kept the lead throughout and won the race easily; fellow front rower Nigel Whorton was not able to keep in touch. Whorton finished second, Bert Finnikin third. It was John's first major championship success and just reward for his great start to the season on tarmac.

With his tarmac car running well, John crossed the Channel for a second trip to Holland and the Long Track Championship. Although John had picked up valuable long track experience the year before, it helped little. He finished in fifth place, the top British driver, but was lapped by the winner. Rien Rutjens won his fifth Long Track World Final in six years and was joined on the podium by the same Dutch drivers with whom he shared it the season before, Friedhelm Welters and Piet Keijzer. Rutjens was a long track specialist racing with Hoosier racing tyres and a small block Chevrolet engine, the leader of a movement in which Dutch cars were becoming more specialised and finely tuned for long track racing. Some began to doubt whether British drivers would ever be competitive at Baarlo again. John looked at the Hoosier racing tyres with an interested eye. It was the first time that he had seen them in race action, and he would remember their effectiveness when he got a chance to test them a few months later.

John's car was still perfect on British tarmac tracks. He won two more meeting finals at Skegness and two at Northampton before his first meeting final victory on shale for the season, at Mildenhall near Bury St Edmunds, a new track that struggled to attract spectators and would close after two years. Eight days later, John won on shale again, in the Grand Prix Series at Sheffield. Those shale victories came in the fortnight before the World Final, a race that would also be held on shale and the main reason why John concentrated on developing a new shale car over the winter.

The host of the World Championship, Belle Vue, was on death row. The Valley Parade fire had put the spotlight on stadium safety and Belle Vue's wooden structure meant that it was declared a fire risk. It was demolished at the end of the season, a sad end for a track that had hosted fourteen World Championships and which generated an atmosphere that was second to none.

The Belle Vue shale was not one of John's best in terms of results. As well as the two races that he won over the Christmas holiday meetings and the 'who dares wins' race in September 1986, John won only a solitary Belle Vue race in the build-up to the 1987 World Final, a heat on 4th May. John found that Nigel Hardy tended to win a lot of finals as a yellow or blue top, and it was difficult to catch him.

This time, however, drivers starting in lower grades would not affect the result by holding up cars behind them because the grid for the most important race of the year was decided by the results of the World Semi-Finals. Having amassed the most points in the qualifying rounds, John started his semi-final at Sheffield on pole. Dave Berresford started alongside on the outside of the front row and got the better start to take the lead through the first corner. John slipped in behind and followed him to the end of the race, happy to secure a berth on the second row in the World Final rather than risking all in a lunge for the win.

Berresford went into the World Final as the pre-race favourite. He had yet to win a major title but the general feeling was that his time had come. Frankie Wainman started alongside him on pole. John started on the inside of the second row with Nigel Whorton next to him. Behind him, on row 3, were Len Wolfenden and Bert Finnikin.

John had a rush to get his car ready for the big race. The day before, at Bradford, Ian Higgins punted John into the fence during the Grand National. It was the latest act in an occasional feud that dated back to 1985 when Higgins buried George Braithwaite in the Aycliffe fence, bending the chassis on the car Braithwaite had borrowed from John. John reignited the conflict two years later when he took out Higgins at Aycliffe on the last corner of the Grand National as he chased maximum points from the meeting, mistakenly thinking that Higgins was in the lead. Higgins returned the favour at Bradford five days later, the eve of the World Championship meeting, shoving John onto the wooden beams on the infield. The steering wheel whipped round and strained John's wrist, forcing him to go to the World Final with it bandaged; but the damage to the car was more serious and the repairs went on late into the night.

The following day the preparation in the Belle Vue pits before the World Final was intense, with mechanics and drivers poring over their cars to check every little detail. Except, it seemed, in the section of the pits by John's car. He arrived at Belle Vue quite early on a damp, drizzly day. A busy night at Bradford and in the workshop a home left John feeling drained and tired – put simply, he was knackered. He retired to the bunk on the transporter bus and slept. That meant he missed both meeting heats, where drivers who did not qualify for the World Final raced to win a place in the meeting final. It also meant that John was unaware of how the cars looked to be handling the track and the weather conditions.

John Dowson returned with his car at the end of the second heat and parked up. John asked him about the condition of the track and was told by Dowson that the rain didn't seem to have affected grip except on one section of the first turn. It was now up to John to select the best tyres. On most shale tracks he raced with three Trakgrip tyres, two on the front axle and one on the inside rear. The outside rear tyre depended on the specific track conditions. If it was dry, he used a RS5 road tyre. In wet conditions, he used an off-road tyre made by Alliance which moved more water from underneath the rubber. Most drivers followed the same pattern of tyre selection. However, John had sussed out over the course of a year or two that even when the shale at Belle Vue dried out a little the Alliance tyre retained grip. Other drivers were less willing to accept that the Alliances performed well in the dry.

So John went onto the grid with an Alliance tyre on his outside rear, confident that it would give him a small advantage when the track was still a little wet at the start, yet still keep grip at the end of the race when the track dried out. John was also confident that Berresford, Wainman and virtually every other car on the grid would run with an RS5 tyre on.

The green flag dropped and the cars roared down the home straight. John kept his foot on the accelerator and eyed up Wainman's rear bumper. As Wainman braked for the first turn, John timed his hit perfectly. Wainman was knocked wide, leaving John just enough room to sneak down the inside. Even better, Wainman's car blocked Berresford's path through the turn and forced him wide through the corner too. Unlike the 1980 World Final, when John smacked Stuart Smith into the fence on the first turn and caused a restart, this time he deftly did enough to get past but without causing carnage. It was skilful, precise driving.

As the cars slid through the first corner, John found that the shale was wet on one section, just like John Dowson had told him. His rear end drifted into some deep shale; the Alliance tyre gripped and shot him down the far straight. Other cars slipped slightly before they accelerated out of the corner. John had created a gap between himself and those following; Wainman and Berresford were already too far away to get an immediate response in. John was in the lead, his unusual tyre choice paying dividends.

John now waited for something to go wrong. He was worried that the track would dry out to the extent that his tyre would begin to slow him down. He was also aware that there were still a couple of dozen cars left on track, any of which could put him out of the race. He tried not to get involved with any backmarkers, but still had to pass them and keep the distance between him and the chasing cars. Although John was being cautious, he also went in hard with his bumper to make sure that no car he passed could return the compliment on the next turn. On one of these occasions John mistimed his hit slightly and his front bumper hooked onto Nigel Hardy's rear bumper. Locked together, the two cars rounded the turn, their speed rapidly falling away. Momentum sheared Hardy sideways down the straight after the turn and John's bumper slid free. He could breathe again. He also had a brief coming together with Willie Harrison, but managed to get away from him too.

The car was flying and the Alliance did not deteriorate at all throughout the race. As the starter signalled the last lap, John was aware that Wainman was half a lap behind. With the understandable caution that strikes a driver who knows he has won a race as long as he gets the car around the track safely, John rounded Belle Vue one last time to pass under the chequered flag. The sense relief in the cab was immeasurable.

He was now the World Champion.

It felt like the hardest race John had ever been part of, but in truth it was a one-car procession from the first turn to the last. Yet it was a race that John would remember fondly for the rest of his life.

The following day John arrived at the traditional post-World Championship meeting at Northampton sporting the coveted gold roof. He failed to finish the final but finished second in his heat to the former World Champion Peter Falding and third in the Grand National. Back on track so soon after the biggest win of his career, John was indicating that it was business as usual even though he was now classed the best driver in the sport. Many drivers over the past decades had crumbled under the pressure of being World Champion. John did not want to be one of them.

There was still the Grand Prix Series to conclude. John topped the standings with two meetings to go, having won four out of the nine rounds so far. After a little wobble in the penultimate meeting at Long Eaton, where he finished seventh in the final, John took second place in the final of the last meeting to win the competition and the prize money that came with it. John's 410 points equated to a meeting average of 36 points over the series, the highest ever recorded, and a safe margin over Len Wolfenden's 384 and Bert Finnikin's 352.

John was striding over the sport like a colossus. By the time he won the Grand Prix Series he had guaranteed victory in the National Points Championship, eventually finishing over 700 points in front of Frankie Wainman and over 1000 points in front of third-placed Bert Finnikin. Not only had John raced the most meetings during the season, he had won double the number of finals than his nearest opponent (14 to Wainman's 7) and had the best meeting average by far (34.75 compared to Finnikin's 27.90).

So John finished the 1987 season holding the three biggest titles in stock car racing: World Champion, National Points Champion and British Champion. He had won all three by a massive margin. The British Championship and World Final were won emphatically, with the second place driver some distance back, and the National Points Championship was as good as over two-thirds of the way through the season. The final meeting of the season also saw John clinch the Grand National Championship for the second season in a row, and he finished second in the Scottish Championship at Newtongrange.

There had been some doubt at the start of the season as to which of the new generation would take on Stuart Smith's mantle as the sport's leading driver. That question had been comprehensively answered now.

Of course, John could not claim to be one of the all-time greatest drivers yet. As if to prove that point, Stuart Smith came out of retirement for the last meeting at Belle Vue before it was demolished and claimed his 500th career final victory to rapturous acclaim. He also beat John in a five-lap race at Hartlepool, where John pitted his Formula 1 car against Smith in a borrowed Formula 2. John wanted to match the Maestro, but he still had plenty to do.

Spot the difference - John and Ian Higgins (29)
in the 1988 World Final

6

Double World Champion
1988

Just as the best drivers from Holland, the USA and New Zealand were invited to compete in the World Final every year, so the best British drivers were now being invited to the flagship event in New Zealand. January 1987 saw the inaugural 240 Championship, named after the 240 cubic inch engines used in Kiwi stock cars. Reigning World Champion Peter Falding was joined by Chris Elwell for the long journey south, and Elwell shocked the hosts by winning the event. The championship was deemed a success despite losing the title to a foreigner, so soon after winning the 1987 World Final John was contacted and asked if he would be prepared to give up three weeks of his winter break to compete in New Zealand. Neither Elwell nor any other driver voiced an interest in joining him, so John was to be the only British representative at the second 240 Championship.

It was a daunting prospect to travel so far and race in an unfamiliar country, but it was an opportunity that could not be turned down. It was impossible for John to ship his stock car such a long way and in any case his own car would not match the different rules and regulations of the New Zealand association. Instead the promoters of the 240 Championship arranged to borrow a car for him. John needed to sort out his own flight and accommodation, although the promoters would reimburse his travel costs. He was given the contact details of a few different drivers in New Zealand and chose to reach out to Graeme Barr, who had raced in the 1986 World Final. John telephoned and found himself in conversation with Barr's mother. Her response was very warm; she said that John and his crew would be welcome to stay with them and they should make themselves known when they arrived in New Zealand. No more advance notice was needed.

A handful of John's mechanics and crew boarded the plane with him and they arrived in Auckland at 11am on Friday morning. It was the same day that the New Zealand Championship, a second major Kiwi championship ranked only behind the 240, was due to be held at Napier. It was there that John had arranged to introduce himself to Peter Pitcher, the promoter who had invited him across. John hired a camper van at the airport and his team piled inside ready to make the 250 mile journey across North Island. The camper van had a wide body with narrow axles and seemed to roll like a ship as it cornered.

The tired crew followed the state highway to Taupo then picked up a road that ran the final two hours to Napier. Glancing at his watch, John realised that they were going to struggle to make it for the start of the meeting. Although he was not scheduled to race, John did not want to create a bad impression by turning up late. Checking the petrol gauge, which showed a quarter of a tank remaining, John decided to skip filling up the tank with diesel at Taupo in favour of filling up further along the road. He soon realised that the New Zealand road network was not like Britain's; the highway disappeared into the forest, trees as far as the eye could see, with no sign of a garage or petrol station. John took to free wheeling downhill to conserve diesel when the petrol gauge warning light illuminated on the dashboard. The camper van must have been running on fumes as it rolled into Napier, and John pulled into the first petrol station that he saw. The attendant gave them directions to Palmerston North stadium and the camper van pulled into the car park just as the meeting began. A highly organised procedure the journey was not, but everything seemed to fall into place to get them there just in time!

John had spent over a decade in British pits and knew all the drivers, mechanics and families. In New Zealand, he didn't know a single person. He watched a couple of races before asking a marshal where he could find Peter Pitcher. The marshal pointed in the direction of the centre green, where Pitcher was in conversation with a fellow promoter, Spike Richardson. They were completely different to the promoters that John knew in Britain, fans as much as businessmen, and placed themselves on the centre green so they could be as close to the action as possible.

Pitcher asked John if he had his helmet with him. He did, it was in the camper van. The promoters then set about finding John a car to drive in the last race of the meeting. Almost before he knew what was happening, John was on the grid behind the wheel of a local stock car. It was a baptism of fire. The car was awful; John was sat uncomfortably upright and the steering wheel was flat like a wagon. The steering barely turned; one rotation took it from one lock to the opposite. The whole setup was unfamiliar and John spent most of the race trying to avoid crashing.

It also felt like most of the native drivers were singling out him for rough treatment, although he later realised that this was just a feature of racing in New Zealand; drivers in the southern hemisphere rarely hesitated to use the bumper to pile an opponent into the fence if an opportunity arose. After the race, John sat back in the seat – as much as it would let him – and wondered what he had let himself in for.

At least the drivers were more welcoming off the track. The local driver who lent John his car told John that both he and Graeme Barr and their respective crews were staying at his house overnight. Barr, the one familiar face who John knew but had failed to find all evening, would be late because he had been sent to hospital after the first race to strap up a dislocated shoulder. John and his crew were ready for a good long sleep, but at the close of the meeting all the drivers and their entourages went to the clubrooms and spent some time at the bar. When they finally got going, in the early hours of the morning, John's crew were so tired that they fell asleep in the camper van, while John drew the short straw and was given the responsibility of driving. It wasn't far, and he parked the camper van on the lawn in the driver's garden. As he mounted the kerb onto the grass the unstable camper van rocked wildly from side to side, but none of the shattered crew woke up. John played the part of the polite guest on his own and went inside for a drink. There he found a bath full of cold water and cans of beer – the night was not over yet!

Another couple of hours passed before John prised himself away from the party and retired to the camper van to sleep. All of the bunks were taken, so he settled down to sleep in the driver's seat. After hours on the plane, a day of driving, a race meeting and a moderate amount of alcohol, John thought that he would have no trouble sleeping. He closed his eyes and managed to doze for a minute or two before the sun rose and streamed through the windscreen, directly onto his face, waking him back up. It was about 4.30 in the morning and John would have to survive on minimal sleep the next day!

John was reacquainted with Graeme Barr, whose arm was in a sling, forcing him to spend some time on the sidelines. Since he was out of action, Barr offered John the use of his stock car rather than the one that the promoters had organised for him. It was completely different to the first one John raced, with a much more familiar cab design and driving position. John spent most of his time in New Zealand working on Barr's car with him, each driver picking up hints and tips from the other. Over the three weekends that John was able to race he gradually fine-tuned Barr's setup to favour his own driving style. He even won a few races as he adjusted to the rough and tumble of New Zealand racing.

The main event was the 240 Championship. Drivers raced in three heats, similarly to the British Championship, each driver starting once at the front, middle and rear of the grid. Unlike the British Championship, however, there was no final champion-ship race and the title was awarded on points accumulated in the heats. John suffered a puncture in his first race, but still managed to finish and picked up some points. In the next race he finished second, in the last he passed the chequered flag first, a long way ahead of the second-placed car. He was so far ahead that the of-ficials did not realise he was in the lead and awarded him a place down the results thinking he was actually a lap behind. Only on the next day, when they reviewed the tapes of the meeting, was the confusion sorted out and John was awarded equal second in the overall standings with Robin Wildbore and Paul Urlich. It was an excellent performance considering that John had not raced in New Zealand before. The title returned to New Zealand, but John had flown the flag for British stock car racing and maintained its reputation.

Although the 240 Championship was John's main reason for travelling to New Zealand, he actually returned with an even greater prize: an innovative addition to his armoury that would help him in the coming season, picked up through one of his old contacts.

When John did not qualify for the 1985 World Final he lent his car to Kiwi driver Ian Easton. On a spare day in his New Zealand holiday, John travelled to meet Easton on his vast wheat farm. Easton was tireless, always on the go, either working hard on his farm or working hard on his stock car. He raced with Hoosier racing tyres, designed specifically for American stock car racing. John questioned Easton about them, having seen them used by Rien Rutjens in Holland but never in Britain before. Easton was an enthusiastic Hoosier advocate and claimed that they far outperformed the cross-ply road tyres that British stock cars used. With typical energy, Easton leapt up and got on the phone to Hoosier's head office in Indiana. He described the situation: he had a British stock car racer who wanted to use Hoosier tyres but didn't have access to them. By an extraordinary quirk of fate the Dutch importer of Hoosiers, Peter Kempen, was sat in the same office in America. He offered to supply John with a few tyres to try out.

John would return to New Zealand a number of times over the following years, but never again would he make such a valuable discovery as those Hoosier tyres. Back in the UK after his travels abroad, John drove to a distribution depot in Bradford to pick up some Hoosiers that Kempen had shipped to him. John eagerly tried them out but was initially disappointed. He was accustomed to using town and country off-road tyres on shale, and the new Hoosiers looked just like normal road pattern tyres. Still, John kept trying with them, mainly on the front axle, and gradually got used to their handling and preparation requirements. Before long, John felt that he had the Hoosiers performing far better than anything that he had managed to achieve with cross-ply tyres and was fitting them on his rear axle too.

The trouble with the New Zealand trip was that it took a big chunk out of the winter, the time that John usually spent building and preparing his cars for the following season. For the first time in a few years he did not build a new car for the new season, instead spending his time perfecting the machines that he had. John was out on track at the first meeting of the season, at Skegness on 6th March, and took victory in heat 1. Although he did not finish the meeting final, John raced in the rest of March like he had never been away. He attended all seven meetings, competing in 21 races in all, and the Skegness final was the only race that he failed to finish. He finished on the podium fifteen times, winning four heats and two finals. The World Champion was out to prove he was not just a one season wonder.

His form continued to impress. May was a particularly strong month in which John won six out of twelve meeting finals, including four consecutively. It was a fabulous run that came to an end just before the British Championship, held on 30th May at Bradford. The defending champion stamped his authority on the meeting from the start by winning heat 1 and went on to win his other two heats, meaning that he was a clear leader in the points and started from pole. The man alongside him, Dave Tapping, earned his place on the front row with positions of first, third and fourth in his heats.

John was the overwhelming favourite to win, but disaster struck in the final. One of the big, wooden beams used as a barrier between the centre green and track was shoved onto the shale by an out of control car. John could not avoid it and ploughed head on into it, his car violently bouncing off. His front wheels and axle were bent and there was no way that he could continue. Dave Berresford avoided the debris and went on to take the win; Willie Harrison was second.

John had lost one of the titles he held, but could make up for that by winning the one that he failed to capture in 1987, the European Championship. This time John finished the race, but agonisingly one place shy of the chequered flag in second. With a quarter of the race to go Jayne Bean looked like she could become stock car's first female champion, leading the race ahead of Frankie Wainman and John. Bean would have been a popular winner, but the hopes of the crowd were dashed when she fell victim to a flat tyre, giving Wainman the lead. John was too far back to challenge and Wainman came home first, winning what would prove to be his last major championship. Paul Harrison, son of Willie, earned his best championship finish in his short career to date by coming home in third.

John's championship race had been a fairly innocuous and safe drive, but the rest of the meeting was anything but. He was on track immediately after the championship race in the first meeting heat, where he was a victim of the unpredictable blue top Richard Pratt. John nudged Pratt wide to overtake him but Pratt responded on the next corner with a huge wallop that nearly sent John through the fence. The race was stopped and it was feared that John was injured, but he was unhurt and leapt out of the cab and towards Pratt's car. Marshals quickly congregated round John, trying to defuse a confrontation. But that was not John's intention. To the delight of the spectators he shook Pratt's hand in a gesture of sportsmanship and walked away. John knew that the gold roof singled him out and he was often a target for aggressive drivers so there was no point in losing his cool. Instead, he logged Pratt's manoeuvre in his memory and waited for a chance to get him back.

The wedged car caused a troublesome extraction job, but the damage wasn't too bad and John was back on track to win the consolation and finish second in the meeting final to Les Mitchell. John then concluded the meeting by giving notice that if you dish it out, you have to learn to take it. On the last lap of the Grand National, as John was on his way to another race win, he saw a lap-down Pratt entering the first turn. John aimed his front bumper, stamped his foot on the accelerator and hit Pratt's backside. A few seconds later John passed the chequered flag and looked at the fence in front of him. Pratt's car was stranded on top of another car, buried deep in the fence; the marshals would need to perform another complicated extraction. The meeting saw John achieve two wins and two seconds in five races; although Wainman left with the European title, John was the undoubted star of the meeting.

Richard Pratt was not the only one who felt John's bumper during the season; John also had a number of battles with Peter Falding. After winning the World Final in 1986, something of a shock result, Falding had dropped off the pace in 1987. Perhaps he tasted success a little too early in his career and struggled to cope with it or perhaps he suffered from the rough treatment other drivers meted out to the World Champion; but in 1988 he was approaching his best and was prepared to trade blows with John. The first sign of this was when a lap down Falding side-swiped John into a pile-up at Crewe to stop him winning the meeting final. John got his own back at Sheffield by dumping Falding on his roof. It was the beginning of a rivalry that would last for six years; as Falding continued to improve he became more of a threat to John.

Conflict was not confined to the track. By the middle of the season, John unwittingly became embroiled in an issue that would divide stock car drivers for the remainder of the decade.

Graham Blundell, a red top driver who had the thankless position as Chairman of the British Stock Car Drivers Association, sidled up to John in the pits to discuss his new tyres. Although John was certain that the Hoosiers complied with all the necessary regulations in terms of their width, size and tread, Blundell reported that a number of drivers were unsure whether they should be classed as legal because they were racing tyres rather than road tyres. He requested that John stop using Hoosiers until the BSCDA had been able to discuss them at their next meeting. Ultimately the tyres were passed as legal and by the time the World Final came around a month or two later John was back using them, but the discontent would continue to simmer as some drivers remained opposed to their use. For those who joined the Hoosier revolution like Joe Jopling, Ray Tyldesley and John Toulson, John took on the responsibility of importing and selling the tyres in the UK for Peter Kempen. That lasted for about twelve months until Kempen wanted John to expand and sell to other motorsport formulas, not just stock cars. Work on the farm came first, so John politely turned down the offer to become Hoosier's permanent UK agent.

Hoosiers were more established in Holland and had received a better welcome there. John put a stash of the tyres in his transporter bus and headed across the Channel for the Long Track Championship, thankful for the chance to have a run out on the new rubber without having to justify their use to a committee.

Along with the other British regulars like Peter Falding, Frankie Wainman and Chris Elwell, John wanted to break Dutch dominance in the Long Track Championship. They succeeded and the trophy did cross the channel, but it went to Rotherham rather than Rimington. John finished second in all three races; the Long Track Championship, Jac Claes Trophy and the meeting final, but it was Falding who took the glory and who beat him on each occasion. Falding had his car set up perfectly for the long straights and he maintained his lead ahead of John with relatively little difficulty on each occasion. Although John was becoming more familiar with the driving style and technique needed to master the long Baarlo circuit, he was still learning. He flooded his engine at the start of the Long Track Championship race and started slowly, recovering to pass Koos Peters with five laps to go for second. By the meeting final John had perfected the last-minute braking that helped drivers circulate the Baarlo at the highest possible speed, but was still unable to reel in the leader. Falding's triumph was the beginning of a five-year period of British success at Baarlo.

A consistently strong showing in the World Championship qualifying rounds meant that John started his World Semi-Final from pole position. Things seemed to be going John's way early in the race. He timed his acceleration from pole position well and kept the lead through the first turn while major rival Nigel Whorton started slowly from row 3 and pulled off with a flat tyre. Then Danny Clarke spun on the second turn and was stranded half on, half off the track. Things got even better for John when, on lap two, Dave Berresford lost time as he slipped sideways as he struggled to defend his line. Ray Tyldesley then exited with a flat tyre.

John had a big lead, but the exit of the cars behind opened the way for Ian Higgins to charge through from row 4. By three-quarters of the way through the race John was slowing while Higgins and Berresford battled for second place. With three laps to go, John came up against a group of cars battling for the last few qualifying positions: Jayne Bean, Richard Pratt, Andy Clarke, Richard Ainsworth and Rod Falding. All three front runners passed Bean but John was slow to do so, allowing Higgins and Berresford to close right up. John then approached Pratt with caution, not wanting to risk the backmarker sending him out on the last lap as payback for the shenanigans at the Northampton meeting a couple of weeks earlier. He hung behind, hoping that Higgins and Berresford would also settle for their places, but Higgins nipped by on the last turn to take the win. John stayed in second, ahead of Berresford. He was still in the World Final, and he would have been happy with second place if it had been offered to him at the start of the race.

Hednesford in Staffordshire was the venue for the World Championships, a windfall for a track that had only returned to the calendar at the start of the season. Hednesford hosted stock cars in the sixties and mid-seventies but for the twelve years that spanned John's career it had been absent from the schedule. On its return, John had to learn how to get round the unique tarmac oval. It was the longest British circuit, with straights that allowed cars to build up a big head of steam and turns that were not slippery like many other tarmac tracks and encouraged high-speed cornering. Whereas most tracks had a limited speed beyond which drivers would lose control, Hednesford allowed them to floor the accelerator on the straights, keep traction as they drifted wide through the corners and be early on the accelerator again to pick up speed on the exit. John picked up the Hednesford technique as quickly as anybody, winning heat 1 in the comeback meeting in March, and winning the meeting final in May and July.

John started the World Final on the inside of the second row, exactly the same position that he won the race from the previous year. Moreover, the same driver was in front of him on pole: Frankie Wainman. Ian Higgins took up his place on the outside of the front row. Peter Falding lined up behind Higgins, to John's right. The danger men in a good position to take out the defending champion on the first turn were Chris Elwell and Dave Berresford on row 3.

Yet the front of the grid nearly had a gaping hole. Higgins nearly didn't make it. He raced in Sheffield the week before but had a serious disagreement with the fence. The car was repaired over next week but a bent distributor drive had gone unnoticed. At the worst possible moment, as it idled towards the scrutineers in the Hednesford pits, the engine seized up.

Two men stepped into the breach. Both Frankie Wainman and John offered Higgins the use of their spare shale cars, generous acts of sportsmanship that were rightly applauded. The choice was easy. John's cars were the best, and Higgins gratefully accepted the offer in return for half of his start money and any winnings. Moreover, giving his spare car to a rival for the title brought to an end the tit-for-tat feud between John and Higgins that had existed since Higgins fenced George Braithwaite in one of John's cars.

There was no repeat of John's relaxed build-up to the previous World Final from his bunk. He arrived the day before the big race to take part in the whole of the two-day World Championship meeting. All drivers were able to take a good look at the track conditions in the full race meeting on the day before the World Final, with two extra races allowing foreign entrants to race for their grid position in the main event. John did not finish the final of the first day's racing, although he was not alone. Few of the top drivers were taking many risks so close to the World Final.

The early season advantage that John had in using Hoosier tyres had worn off. Other drivers flocked to buy them from John as soon as the BSCDA passed them for use, and as the cars lined up in the pits before the World Final John could see that most of the top drivers had Hoosiers fitted. John was waiting in the car to be called out on the track when one of Len Wolfenden's former mechanics approached him. John was expecting him to wish good luck, but the mechanic had something more ominous to say: John's inside rear tyre was going flat. Charging back to his transporter bus, John realised that he did not have another Hoosier ready on a wheel. He was forced to swap the Hoosier from the outside of the rear axle to the inside and put a recapped cross-ply tyre on the outside. Back in the pit queue, sat in his car's cab, John settled himself for the big race. If his preparation for the previous World Final had been overly-relaxed, this time it was overly-frantic!

When the green flag dropped, the cars raced away. The first lap saw both John and Peter Falding get past Frankie Wainman and Ian Higgins to take the first two places. The two front runners then danced around the track, swapping the lead between them. Falding nudged John wide to take first place, but John recovered his line and slipped in behind Falding. Then John retook the lead by knocking Falding wide, but Falding returned the compliment and the lead switched again. When Roger Warnes spun and Falding had to take evasive action, John closed right up and followed Falding round the track. This time, John was determined to take the lead and keep it. On lap 10 he hit Falding into the fence, winding him and buckling his wheel. Falding carried on but dropped back, eventually finishing in fifth place. John's only real threat was gone. Ian Higgins finished fourth, Chris Elwell third and John Toulson second. John crossed the line first, becoming a double World Champion.

The cross-ply tyre on the outside rear had surprisingly good grip and speed, although by the end the recapped surface was beginning to overheat. As John trundled back to the pits, a big blister developed on the rubber. Whether the car would have had the same speed with two Hoosiers on the rear axle, John would never know – perhaps he got lucky and the cross-ply actually gave a better performance that the Hoosier would – but it is clear that the recapped cross-ply would not have survived had the race lasted another five laps.

When he won the World Championship the previous year, John was one of 24 drivers who had claimed the gold roof. This time he had entered a more privileged club. Only four drivers had won the World Championship twice: Johnny Brise, Fred Mitchell, Dave Chisholm and Stuart Smith. Now John Lund was added to that elite group.

Even though there were two months left to run in the season, John was far clear of the field in the National Points Championship. It allowed him to take a week or two out to celebrate being a double World Champion, and a couple of weeks later, being a double dad. Sam was born at the end of the month, a second son for John and Sarah.

The pressure was off; both gold and silver roof were in the bag. John also claimed first place in the Grand Prix Series with third place in the final of the last meeting of the series at Coventry, having won the rounds at Hednesford, Bradford and Northampton and finished second at Skegness and Mildenhall. He then won a third consecutive Grand National Championship, leading from pole position in the championship race at Sheffield. At that same meeting he won his heat and the meeting final too, and came home second in the Grand National; Ian Higgins narrowly beat John to the chequered flag to stop him scoring a maximum.

Winning the heat, final and Grand National in a meeting was always the sign of a driver in top form. It required consistent speed and skill to win a heat and final in the same meeting. Then, since the meeting final winner started the Grand National a lap down, an extra slice of luck was required to make it three wins in three races. John went close to the maximum again at the meeting after the Grand National Championship, winning heat and final at Crewe but finishing second in the Grand National to Bert Finnikin. Nigel Whorton also tripped John at the last hurdle, at Coventry on 4th June, beating John into second in the

Grand National after John had won heat and the final. It was a meeting which John left sorely disappointed since the starter indicated that he was the leading car with a third of the race to go. The mistake meant that John was unaware that Whorton was actually half a lap in front of him and he throttled back and raced for what he thought was an easy victory. When the chequered flag waved in front of Whorton as the race ended, the air turned a shade of blue inside John's cab.

That still left four occasions where John did score the maximum points available: at Long Eaton on 14th May, Northampton on 29th May, and twice at Bradford, on 25th June and 29th August. The Northampton meeting, on wet tarmac, was a particularly strong performance where John seemed to be driving a car that had an extra ten miles an hour compared to his opponents. He swiftly made up the lap disadvantage in the Grand National and overtook Graham Blundell, Frankie Wainman and Nigel Whorton before passing John Cayzer in a last-bend finale. At one of the Bradford maximums, John was pleased to spot his parents in the crowd. They were making a rare visit to watch their son, eager to see what all the fuss was about, and dashed along the M62 after milking the cows. They went away realising that their son had improved beyond recognition from the other times they had seen him race, at Nelson when John was first starting out. Then, John was chaotic and unpredictable. Now it looked like John's car was on rails, circling the track effortlessly, while those around him struggled for grip.

Of course, not everything went John's way. For two years he had dominated at Aycliffe, but in 1988 he was challenged by John Toulson, who won five meeting finals to John's two. However, the Aycliffe results were part of a bigger picture. John had moved on from dominating at just a few tracks that suited his style and car. In 1987, half of his meeting final victories came at Aycliffe;

the other eight were split between five tracks. In 1988, John won consistently across the country, on both shale and tarmac. His best track was Northampton, with six meeting final victories, but over the course of the season John won meeting finals at eleven different venues.

Not surprisingly, when the end of season points were totted up John was top of the grading list with 3352 points, ahead of Frankie Wainman on 2064 and Ray Tyldesley with 1456. John had won 25 meeting finals, comprehensively beating his total of fourteen the year before, and had won 101 races compared to 53 the year previous. There was no doubt that 1988 was John's finest season so far, but it was also one of the most dominant seasons by a single driver in the history of the sport.

Frankie Wainman was beginning to drop off the pace. Although he remained second in the National Points Championship, comfortably ahead of the next pack of drivers, he won only six meeting finals during the season and would not win another for the next twelve years. Wainman's time was being spent preparing for the next generation. His son, Frankie Wainman Junior, finished eleventh in the grading list at the end of his first full season. The new Wainman, benefiting from his father's vast experience in car preparation, won two finals and even scraped onto the podium in the British Championship. He was the first indication that there was a new generation of drivers coming through.

With Stuart Smith gone and Frankie Wainman on the wane, John was now the old guard, fighting to retain his now undisputed status as the top driver in the sport.

Lining up at Baarlo in 1990, shadowed by a youthful
Paul Harrison (22)

7

Long Track Champion
1989-90

A little fame came the way of the double World Champion at the start of 1989. John travelled to a television studio to take part in Tell The Truth, a show presented by Fred Dinenage. A panel of four celebrities; Roy Hudd, Barbara Dickson, Bob Wellings and Kathy Taylor, had to pick the real stock car champion from a selection of three possibilities. Each of the potential John Lunds wore an orange fire-proof driving suit and had to answer questions fired at them by the panel. John's casual, easy-going nature gave him away; 'the quietest chap has got to be it', and all four celebrities correctly identified him. It saved John from a ribbing in the pits – it would have been quite embarrassing if the two other men, both vicars, were seen as more likely stock car drivers!

The brief television appearance fitted around a busy winter. The World Final win in 1988 meant that John was invited to race in New Zealand a second time, and he was joined on the long journey by the stock car racing Dorrell family; Peter, Clinton and Shane, and Formula 2 racer Russell Taylor. None of the other British drivers had John's stature or reputation, so the burden of British hopes rested on his shoulders.

John started the 240 Championship well, winning his first heat from the third row of the grid in a car loaned from Clinton MacDonald and avoiding the typical Kiwi bumper work that put out many of his opponents. The second race saw John on the tenth row of the grid and with more to do if he was to stay at the top of the points table, but he justified his World Champion tag with a strong drive that saw him take victory ahead of Graeme Barr. With two of the three races gone, John had a maximum of 52 points; Barr was second in the standings with 48.

The third race was the decider. John started in the middle of the grid and needed to avoid being taken out by the Kiwis. He survived the majority of the race unscathed, although he was under constant attack from local drivers who wanted to see one of their own win the title. By the last lap John worked himself into a position where he should win, but he carried a little too much speed into the penultimate corner and drifted wide. That was all the invitation necessary for Dave Evans, who fired into John's back end and ploughed him into the fence. At almost exactly the same time, a rollover came to rest a few metres away.

Red flags waved, but John was already out of the race and his championship hopes had gone. Only later was it realised that the race had gone on a lap too long. When the starter indicated one lap to go, he should actually have been waving chequered flag. The officials rejected John's protest and kept the declared result with the positions as they were when the red flags were waved, leaving John out of the race in sixth place in the final champion-ship standings.

The carnage on the last lap left John rueing the brutal racing tactics on the other side of the world, where drivers were prepared to sacrifice their own race in order to help another driver pick up a decent position. However, he was more annoyed with the deci-sion of the officials. John claimed that he was fenced after the race should have ended and that the result should have amended to that which stood when the intended race distance was completed, making him the winner. It looked suspiciously like the officials were purposely handing the title to a New Zealander by saying that the extra lap was part of the race. But John remained the moral victor, having come so close to championship success in an unfamiliar car on an unfamiliar track.

John returned from New Zealand and rushed to prepare his cars for the first race meetings of the season. It was a busy few weeks in the workshop and there were many late nights. He had sold his shale car, the 1987 World Final winner, to Pete Bashford at the end of the previous season. John wanted to build a new tarmac car, so his existing three-year-old tarmac car was converted for shale use. The new tarmac car sported a new gearbox and bon-net design to save weight and minor amendments to the degree of chassis offset to slightly adjust weight distribution. It was powered by a new tall-block Bowtie Chevrolet engine.

John also tried to keep up with the orders that were coming his way from other drivers. They recognised that John's cars were the best on track and had begun to examine them as closely as possible in the pits to see where the advantage came from. Murray Harrison started 1989 with a chassis purchased from the Lund workshop, while Willie and Paul Harrison each constructed their own cars based on the Lund design.

This was all on top of the regular farm work. The start of the stock car season also coincided with the lambing season, meaning that there were many overnight shifts and a lack of time to dedicate to pre-season preparations. Norman and Brenda made way for John and his young family, moving to a house about a mile down the road while John, Sarah, James and Sam moved into the farm. Although Norman was still an active part of the farm and would continue to be so for another two decades, John was now the man on the spot. It was his responsibility to ensure than the milking was done every morning and evening, and that all the necessary jobs were completed each day to enable the farm continued to turn over a profit.

The workload meant that the new tarmac car was not ready for the start of the season and John's shale car was forced to double-up on both surfaces during the first three months, but despite running a single car he started strongly. A solitary meeting final victory in March, at Bradford, was backed up with seven other race wins. John's main rival was Peter Falding, and great races like the meeting finals at Crewe on 15th April and Northampton on 16th April were an early sign that it was to be a scrap at the top of the grading list. John steadily improved in April with three final victories and four other race wins. By the time the British Championship came around on 27th May he was flying again, with five final victories and seven other race wins in the month to that point.

John qualified well in his heats at the British Championship, finishing fourth, third and first in his heats, but he was just one of a group of drivers who dominated the heats: Dave Berresford, Danny Clarke and Richard Dobson each won two, Peter Falding finished first, second and third, while Bert Finnikin had two second place finishes. So it was a strong clutch of in-form drivers who formed the first few rows of the grid for the championship race. John was on row 2 with Berresford, while the front row was reserved for Falding and Clarke.

Falding and John led the way after the first lap bumper work, while Berresford and Clarke slipped back after clashing on the second lap. On the third lap John eased Falding aside and took the lead, pulling clear and giving himself breathing space. John and Falding both raced away from the rest of the field, their nearest challenger a distant Ray Tyldesley. John kept in front of Falding to pass the chequered flag first, winning the British Championship for a second time. Clarke was the only other driver who started on the front three rows to finish in the top ten, in ninth place; Berresford, Dobson and Finnikin failed to cross the line.

Behind the scenes, arguments about tyres continued to rumble on. John had been joined by many other drivers in using Hoosiers, but there were a few remaining who refused to accept that racing tyres should be used on stock cars. The BSCDA committee banned road tyres with a width of greater than six and a half inches and town and country pattern tyres with a width greater than seven and a half inches. While this didn't ban Hoosiers outright, it did mean that the Hoosiers used by John in 1988 were no longer legal. The fudge was made even less clear when drivers were allowed to use up their stocks of old Hoosiers at selected meetings before the end of June, by which time Hoosier had come up with an alternative tyre that matched the new criteria. Ray Tyldesley also found that McCreary racing tyres were legal under the new regulations and supplied them as a suitable alternative. The rule changes did nothing to solve the fundamental issue: should racing tyres be allowed on stock cars?

In an ideal world John would happily have stuck with crossply tyres, but they were too difficult and expensive to get hold of. They were originally manufactured for heavy cars made by Rolls-Royce, Bentley and Rover, but those cars were disappearing from the roads and their tyres were increasingly difficult to source. Supply and demand meant that the price shot up and it was cheaper to race with imported Hoosiers. A Dunlop RS5 tyre cost £120; John could source a Hoosier for half the price. Dunlop Weathermasters were even harder to find. Nigel Hardy, John's best source for tarmac-ready Weathermasters, had retired at the end of 1988 and John no longer had his shale-raced cast-off tyres to use on tarmac. Shale tyres were becoming scarce too. Town and country pattern tyres were becoming more difficult to trace as the market that they were produced for – the affluent Rolls Royce owners who drove on dust roads in the Middle East – began to produce tyres themselves rather than importing UK-produced rubber.

A few hunted for a compromise solution. Some drivers tried radial tyres, but they were unsuitable and results were poor. Others tried to rely on recapped rubber on old tyre casings, the kind of tyre that John had fitted at the last minute in the 1988 World Final, but the variable quality of the rubber compounds and workmanship meant that the cap would often begin to lift off mid-race.

So something had to happen. There were plenty of drivers unhappy, but few offered a real and practical solution. John was convinced that racing tyres like Hoosier were the only option. He avoided the arguments and kept a low profile in the BSCDA meetings, waiting for the ructions to die down. They inevitably did, and more and more drivers joined the Hoosier revolution, but the grumbles continued throughout the season.

The European Championship neatly illustrated the substantial influence tyres could have on results. John debuted his long-awaited new tarmac car, but more important would be his tyre choice since the long Hednesford oval was hard on tyres. By the time the championship was held on 11th June, drivers had begun to sort through the different alternatives and find their preferred tyres. John gambled by opting for US-imported recapped tyres that Mike James had found for him. By saving them for a major championship meeting, John was holding an ace card up his sleeve, but could not tell exactly how well they would perform in the big race.

All qualifying drivers were asked to race in two heats to make up a grid for the championship race. John's two second places were enough to get him on the front row, although pole position was given to Ray Tyldesley who finished first and third. Peter Falding was one half of row 2, alongside Andy Webb.

John took advantage of the clear space ahead of him to accelerate away from the front row and leave a safe gap behind. Falding moved through to take second place, but was struggling with McCreary tyres and could not find the speed to keep up with the leader. Falding waited, biding his time for a late challenge and hoping that John's tyres would deteriorate. They did not; the recaps performed well on this occasion. Falding had misjudged his ability to close the gap and John found it relatively simple to maintain his quarter-lap lead over the last few laps. For the second time in a championship race that season, John steered his car home in first place ahead of Peter Falding. Nigel Whorton had come through from row 6 to take third place, while the other two starters on the first two rows, Ray Tyldesley and Andy Webb, finished fourth and fifth.

John had claimed the only major title that had so far eluded him: he was the European Champion. Since he was also the British Champion, commentators began to consider the possibility that he might go one better than the spectacularly successful 1987 season. If John could win the World Championship and National Points Championship again, he would win all four major championships in one year.

There was also the Dutch-based Long Track Championship to take into account too. John was a strong contender for the title after finishing second there in three races the previous year. He also had the new tarmac car which had just won the European Championship at Hednesford, the most similar track to Baarlo on the British schedule. However, although it all looked good on paper, John failed to make the first all-British Long Track podium since 1979. Sitting behind Peter Falding at the end of the first lap, John moved up from third to second as initial leader Piet Keijzer retired. John knew that this year his new, lightweight, Bowtie Chevy tarmac car had the speed to keep up with Falding, and waited for the right moment to challenge.

As John readied himself for a last lap attack, both he and Falding went into the penultimate corner behind a rapidly-slowing Martin Verhoef, whose water pump had broken. The fan blades in Verhoef's pump sheared through coolant pipes in the engine, spraying oil on the track. Falding lost control and hit the fence, but the force went through the car at a right angle and he did not sustain damage. John could not keep the car level with the fence and flipped onto his roof, then was joined upside-down by the next car, Gary Maynard. Red flags were waved, but the track was so slippery that even slow-moving cars slid into the pile-up. With so little distance left to race and the surface needing treatment to remove the oil, the result was announced as the positions which stood when the red flags were waved. Falding retained the title with Chris Elwell second and Nigel Whorton third.

The trouble was that stock car racing was not a predictable sport. No matter how overwhelming a favourite John might be before a race, he could not factor for mechanical problems or the actions of another driver. The same lesson repeated itself a couple of weeks later. Qualifying for the World Final seemed pre-ordained. John was allocated the World Semi-Final at Aycliffe, his most productive track, and he started from pole position, just as he had for the last two years. John started well and built up a strong lead from Dave Berresford, but after five laps his gearbox shaft broke. With no drive to the wheels, John could do nothing but coast to the centre green, watched by a shocked crowd. The fault was not terminal, John had a new part fitted in time to finish second in the meeting consolation and win the meeting final in two highly-charged drives that gave away how frustrated he was. But John's chance of winning three consecutive World Championships had disappeared, ruined by mechanical failure.

It was the first season where a new Consolation Semi-Final enabled two drivers to win a spot on at the back of the World Final grid, and a week later Frankie Wainman and Dave Berresford were the lucky recipients of a second chance. John already had his. As the reigning champion, he was allowed to start on the back row of the grid even if he didn't qualify for the World Final. The consolation race was left to the other unlucky non-qualifiers to fight it out.

Starting from 31st place on the World Final grid at Coventry, John recognised that a miracle was required if he was to win. Although there was a mid-grid pile-up that left some cars out of the race and others stuck trying to disentangle themselves, losing valuable time, it was not enough for John to make up enough places. By the time John had negotiated his way through the carnage, pole-sitter Ray Tyldesley was already just off his back bumper and John was almost a lap down. Tyldesley kept his momentum going to pass John, who spent the rest of the race sitting just behind. Tyldesley could not ask for a better wing-man. John saw little need to bash the leader out of the way and seemed happy to follow Tyldesley around the track. Falding, in second place, had his biggest rival between him and the World Final leader. He was wary of passing John, expecting that if he did so John would wallop him into the fence. Falding decided to bide his time. He would attack with two laps to go, and when he did so he would hit hard enough to put both John and Tyldesley out of the race.

It was not John but a different backmarker that scuppered Falding's plan. Martin Verhoef cut in front of Falding as he was being lapped, buckling Falding's wheel and forcing him to settle for second. He continued following John and Tyldesley for the rest of the race, Tyldesley took the chequered flag and the gold roof for the next year. John was next to pass the chequered flag but only in tenth place, the first lapped backmarker. Falding may have felt that John had purposely prevented him from having a chance to take the World Final, but John did not have the speed to overtake Tyldesley without smacking him out of the race, and being a lap down, he was not prepared to do that.

The next day, John turned out for the Northampton meeting with a new paint job. The gold roof was absent from his car for the first time in two years, replaced with silver paint, the colour signifying the National Points Champion. It was some time since the silver roof had last been seen on track since John had won the points race for the last two years, and it was the first time that car 53 had raced under silver.

Whether he would lose that honour at the end of the season remained to be seen. Whereas John had been far ahead in the grading list after the World Championship the previous year, this year he was being pushed hard by Peter Falding. The challenger held a narrow lead in the first published points table in May. Every race meeting counted, and as John continued to grind out meeting victories; three in June, three in July, four in August; he was matched by Falding who gained three final victories in June, four in July and three in August.

Falding was determined and stubborn in his chase for the National Points title, and would settle for a podium place if he deemed it more beneficial to the grading list. As early as Skegness on 14th May, Falding was prepared to settle for third in the meeting final, aware that John was out of the race. John found it harder to accept anything less than first, which made for great entertainment as he pushed for the front, but it could also damage his position in the grading list if he overstretched himself. At Northampton on 30th April, John fought for the lead on the last corner despite having a flat tyre, knocking both Gaz Bott and himself out of the race, handing an easy and unexpected win to Falding. Such points were a free handout to John's rival.

The scene was set for a spectacular finish when John won the final at Bradford on 30th September (and in doing so also won the BriSCA Supreme Championship) and Hednesford on 8th October. It gave him the lead in the grading list for the first time during the season, a narrow 71-point advantage. That was followed by a poor middle of the month, with John failing to finish the meeting finals at Northampton, Crewe and Skegness, handing initiative back to Falding. Falding had a great weekend at the end of the month, winning two finals in two days at Bradford and Aycliffe, John in second place each time.

John won heat and Grand National and finished third in the final at Coventry on 4th November, but just as importantly Falding finished second in all three races. John needed to create a gap between himself and the man chasing him in the grading points. He managed it the following day in the last ever meeting at Aycliffe. It was a bittersweet moment; John was sad to see a track go that had served him so well over the past three years, but was happy to win the final and the Grand National Championship at the last meeting.

The Grand Prix Series finished on the Saturday of the penultimate weekend of the season with both John and Falding losing out to Len Wolfenden, who had returned to stock car racing in

1989 and had found his old form again in the second half of the season. The series went down to the final round with John pushing Wolfenden hard, but Wolfenden needed only to finish the final to ensure victory in the overall standings. He managed that, taking third place, while John was stuck in fifth. Although he missed out on the series cash prize, John was happy the next day with wins in the heat and final at Northampton.

John went into the final weekend of the season a week later with a 71 point lead at the top of the grading list. As a reward for the nail-biting conclusion to the season, promoter Keith Barber added an extra £500 to the £1000 prize for the National Points Championship. John and Falding sportingly agreed that whoever won the championship, the extra money would be split between them both. John did enough at Scunthorpe and Hednesford to maintain the gap, and the season finished with him accumulating 3278 points. Falding hadn't quite done enough to overhaul him and finished with 3209; Ray Tyldesley was some way back on 2078.

John kept the silver roof for another year, a consolation for losing the gold one, but he had missed out on the opportunity to join Dave Chisholm and Stuart Smith by winning the World Championship three times in a row. Yet John still had plenty of stock car trophies. He would go into the next season as the National Points Champion, British Champion and European Champion.

The merry-go-round of tracks meant that, as well as Aycliffe, Sheffield was absent from the calendar for the 1990 season. To plug the gaps there were new tracks that welcomed stock cars. Birmingham and Boston hosted their first meetings in 1989, and they were joined the following year by Buxton. The Boston shale would last only four years until developers moved in to demolish the stadium, but the tarmac at Birmingham and Buxton became long-term homes for the sport. John's workshop also resembled a merry-go-round. A new tarmac car was added to the collection; the old tarmac car which had only seen half a season of racing was converted to shale.

In order to bring a bit of life into the first half of the season which was usually spent building up grading and qualifying points, a new championship was held at Northampton on 30th April. The UK Open Championship, as the name suggested, was open to any driver who wished to enter, so qualifying rounds or grading points were not necessary. Drivers raced in two of four heats to create a grid for the final. The front row of the main race was led by John and Ian Higgins, who each won two heats. Higgins was using part-worn tyres while John had fresh rubber, so Higgins intended to nail John on the first bend to try and stop him getting away. John was aware that he was most vulnerable at the start and floored the accelerator on the home straight, already too far in front for Higgins to connect on the first turn. John drove on for an easy victory, Peter Falding pushed through from row 2 for second and Higgins hung on for third. John picked up yet another championship trophy for his collection, but he would soon have to give one of them back. Six days later the European Championship was held at Skegness. A disappointed John trailed in seventh place; Mike James stood on top of the podium.

John won four meeting finals in the first two months of the season, one of which was the UK Open Championship. That was a questionable start to the season by the high standards John had set himself over the last three years. Had Peter Falding not chosen to cut back on racing so he could concentrate on renovating his house and building cars for other drivers, it is likely that John would have slipped from top spot in the grading list. Instead John had a slender lead ahead of Bobby Burns and Paul Harrison, but by mid-May John was starting to hit his stride again. Things turned for the better at Crewe on 19th May, when John ran home ahead of Rob Pearce. That was soon followed by three consecutive meeting final victories; at Bradford, Buxton and Coventry. Those results pushed him clear of the chasing pack at the top of the points table.

Hednesford was the host of the British Championship on 8th July. John went there with good form at the track, although nursing a few bruises from a rollover sustained the previous day at Coventry. His heat results of second, first and first were good enough for a front row start in the main event, but not pole: Chris Elwell, downgraded to blue top for the first time in years, took advantage of his grid position to win all three of his heats and started from pole in the championship race. Danny Clarke, Bert Finnikin and Frankie Wainman were hovering in the rows behind, looking to take advantage of a poor start.

It didn't matter how well a driver performed in the heats if he could not match it in the championship race. John could vouch for that - he had won all three heats in the British Championship in 1988 but failed to finish the final. The same misfortune befell Elwell on this occasion. Elwell started brightly, surging into the lead, whereas John was sluggish and let Clarke past for second. Trying to make up for his poor start, John sent Clarke careering into Elwell on the next turn. The hit created enough of a pile-up to restart the race and caused so much damage to Elwell's car that he retired. Finnikin was also missing when the green flags dropped a second time, creating extra space at the front of the grid. John made no mistake on the restart and took the lead, holding it all the way through the race, followed by Paul Harrison. John may have lost the European Championship, but he had retained the British.

The route to the World Final began at Long Eaton, where John started the World Semi-Final on pole. Des Chandler bungled his gear changes from the outside of the front row, giving John an easy run into the lead. He struggled to stay there, however, having some issues finding grip on the shale. Danny Clarke took the lead after one and a half laps before Paul Harrison went through for second after six laps. John looked at risk of slipping further back at halfway through the race as the cars behind him began to close the gap, but he was a lucky beneficiary when John Toulson ended up sideways across the track in the middle of a corner. Clarke took the outside line but shunted Toulson's back end, while Harrison tried to go on the inside and hit Toulson's front. The three cars veered onto the centre green and John went through to retake the lead. Still struggling, John did not put up much of a fight when Dave Berresford appeared behind him at three-quarter distance. Berresford pushed by to take first place; John settled for second. Berresford's win gave him pole position for the World Final, another chance to win the title that he desperately sought; John was still in the mix on the second row after being unusually off the pace.

After the World Semi-Final, John returned to Holland for another go at the Long Track Championship. This time he was right on the pace. The tarmac car ran perfectly, with barely a missed beat throughout the whole weekend meeting. Starting the championship race from the inside of the third row of the grid, John took a good line through the first turn and immediately promoted himself to third place behind Rob Visscher and Piet Keijzer. At the end of the far straight on the second lap John moved into second, knocking Keijzer against the fence to give him room to move through the inside. Two laps later a nudge to Visscher's rear put John into first. That left John the majority of the race to round the circuit, watching his line. Second-placed Ron Kroonder was never more than a few car lengths behind, ready to take advantage of any slip up, but John scythed through the traffic with no problems. Only on the final turn was there a moment of panic. John slowed to make sure he got round safely and allowed Kroonder to close up. A stomp on the accelerator saw John maintain his lead on the home straight to the chequered flag.

John was a world champion once again. Admittedly the Long Track World Championship did not have the same status as the short track World Final, but it was still a championship meeting in which he had to beat the Dutch in their own backyard and the elite UK drivers.

Even as he clutched the Long Track Championship trophy for the first time, John's attention was shifting back across the channel to the other World Championship, the one that he most coveted. Concerned by the form of his shale car in the World Semi-Final, John made a brave decision. Since the tarmac car had run so well at Baarlo, John decided to save it for the World Final at Bradford, even though the Odsal track was shale. It was put back on the transporter bus and left in his workshop for the next three weeks. John used the shale car at all the meetings between the Long Track Championship and World Final, whether shale or tarmac. That decision would come to haunt him.

At the biggest race of the year, John lined up on the outside of the second row, behind defending champion Ray Tyldesley and alongside Peter Falding, with Dave Berresford on pole. Dutchman Piet Keijzer and New Zealander Paul Urlich were the foreign entrants on row 3, separating the front men from Des Chandler, Bert Finnikin, Ian Platts and Frankie Wainman.

The Bradford shale was wet and greasy at the start of the World Final, so it was difficult to put enough power down to blast round the turns at speed. John's tarmac car coped excellently with the tricky conditions. Starting from the second row, he maintained a gap in front of Chandler, Barry Hunter and Finnikin but behind Berresford, Tyldesley and Falding as the green flag waved. Tyldesley challenged for the lead on the second lap, but in doing so went wide with Berresford and left enough of a gap for Falding and John to breeze into first and second. John then made a move on lap 3, pushing Falding into the loose shale and squeezing round the inside. As he passed the starter for the fourth time, John led from Falding, Berresford and Tyldesley.

John's lead extended slightly when Falding retired with a flat tyre, but the gap was cut eight laps in when Russell Taylor crashed halfway down the far straight and flames were seen underneath his car. Waved yellow flags paused the race to allow Taylor to exit safely, bringing the field closer together. The restart, as always, left the leader vulnerable. John protected his back end and kept the lead, then built up a healthy gap again when Tyldesley followed Falding's example and retired from second place with a flat tyre.

The shale dried out as the drivers circled the track and the laps counted down, allowing the speed of the cars to increase. All, that is, except John's. He seemed to be getting slower and slower. The new second-place driver, Bert Finnikin, closed up and pressured John for a couple of laps. This was not like the World Semi-Final, where John was prepared to let Berresford through and settle for second. This was the World Final, and John was going to force Finnikin to earn the lead. With eight laps remaining, Finnikin pushed John wide and passed him through the turn. John caught back up to him on the next bend but had to go flat out to do so. He got close enough to give Finnikin a push wide, bouncing him off the fence, but John was so committed to the shove that he followed Finnikin wide. It was not enough to retake first place, and the move allowed Berresford to catch up to the front pair. With two laps to go, John was hit from behind and Berresford got past in a perfect copy of Finnikin's manoeuvre. Again John could not get close enough to retake the position.

Finnikin led to the end of the race, Berresford followed him in for second and John took third. It was a frustrating experience. John's car was brilliant at the start, easily quick enough to win, but did not have enough power at the end. The engine began to smoke as it crawled back to the pits, a sign that something was wrong. A thorough inspection afterwards showed that the cylinder rings were worn and the pistons were sticking, causing a loss of compression and power. The long straights at Baarlo had taken their toll and fuel starvation damaged the pistons. John would doubtless have noticed the problem had he raced the car at one of the meetings in between the Long Track Championship and the World Final, but since he had thought that the car was working fine he made only the adjustments to the gearing necessary for Bradford and left the rest of the engine largely untouched. It was a mistake that probably cost him the World Final.

John had a point to prove for the rest of the season. Bert Finnikin wore the gold roof, but John still had the silver roof and wanted to show that he was the most consistently successful driver. Despite the engine trouble, John managed to shepherd his car home third in the meeting final of the World Championship meeting, and also took third place in the meeting final the following day at Northampton. September was rounded off with a disappointing non-finish at Scunthorpe and another third place at Buxton.

With a miserable September out of the way, John began a remarkable run of results in meeting finals in October. He finished first at Coventry despite badly gashing a finger, a wound which would hinder his ability to drive for the next couple of weeks. That makes it all the more impressive that John won the next meeting final at Skegness and came second at Boston, both on the day after the Coventry injury. After that he won three consecutive meeting finals, at Northampton, Crewe and Hednesford, before rounding off October with a third place at Bradford and second at Hartlepool.

It left no doubt that the silver roof would remain on car 53. John finished with 2783 points, far ahead of Bobby Burns' 1856 and Paul Harrison's 1836. John also tied up victory in the Grand Prix Series and won the Grand National Championship yet again, the fifth season in a row. John inherited the lead in that race courtesy of a smooth drive at Crewe when Ian Higgins and Bert Finnikin made mistakes that gave them punctures. John lost the lead with five laps to go when Dave Berresford made up considerable ground and sneaked by. John had been unusually unhurried to that moment, but Berresford spurred him into action and made him work for the win. A trademark Lund lunge on the final lap was enough to get the lead back; Berresford recovered for second.

Although the World Championship had evaded him again, there was little doubt that John was the best driver on track. He was still the National Points Champion, British Champion and Long Track Champion, as well as holder of a host of minor titles. Much as Stuart Smith was recognised as the best driver in the seventies even though the gold roof kept slipping from him, few drivers or spectators would deny that John was the favourite to win almost every race that his car trundled out for. Yet his hunger for the World Championship remained unsatisfied, and John still felt that he had plenty to prove.

The man they all want to beat relaxes
before the 1992 World Final

8

Six-Time Silver
1991-92

The sign of a determined sportsman is one who looks to improve even when he is already the best. John looked back on 1990 and decided that the weakest link in his dominant season was on shale. His 1989-built car, initially used for tarmac, seemed to lack something when he converted it for shale. Struggling to put his finger on the problem, John decided to put the car to one side and made it known that he was prepared to sell it. He spent the winter building a replacement.

The season opened with a double-header at Skegness and Boston on Sunday 3rd March. The new shale car had an immediate impact with heat and final wins at Boston. That victory was part of a strong start to the season which saw John win five meeting finals in March, but he dropped off the pace with only a single final win in April. When the first grading list was published towards the end of April, John held a slim 51 point gap at the top ahead of Peter Falding, who was back competing regularly. Neutrals hoped that 1991 would see a similar tight season-long race for the silver roof between the two drivers as there was in 1989.

Still the tyre dispute rumbled on. John was always looking to get the best out of his tyres and was concerned that his stock of Hoosier F70s were not lasting long enough on the more abrasive tarmac tracks like Hartlepool and Hednesford. He sought a new, harder compound. The Hoosier TD was the result, a tyre which lasted longer at optimum performance and performed equally well at other tarmac tracks. The BSCDA committee still viewed racing tyres with suspicion and they responded by banning the Hoosier TD from 1st April. That did not go down well in the pits. Nine drivers, including John, were disqualified from a Grand National at Hednesford for using illegal Hoosiers in a coordinated protest after the ban came into force. Their actions pressured the BSCDA committee to reverse the decision, allowing the Hoosier TD to be raced until the end of the season, but the dispute led to the resignation of BSCDA chairman Frankie Wainman and vice-chairman Dave Cusack.

Although John was a supporter of the Hoosier TD, the new tyre actually harmed him in the long run. The rubber compound was so durable that it wasn't significantly different whether it was brand-new or partly worn, meaning that the skill of tyre choice and preparation – something that John excelled at – became increasingly irrelevant. Perhaps that helps to explain John's disappointment at the British Championship on the Buxton tarmac on 2nd June. John went there having gained three more meeting final wins in May but all were on shale, including a third win at Boston in three months. Torrential afternoon rain meant that tyre choice was even more important at Buxton. John finished fifth and sixth in two of his heats and failed to finish the third so he started the championship race well down the grid on row 7. Paul Harrison led the way from pole to the chequered flag, winning his first major championship. John came home in fifth.

Seven days after the British Championship, John won a meeting final at Hartlepool, but that was to be his only meeting victory until his next major title chance, the European Championships at Northampton on 21st July. Even more concerning, John won only three other races in the same seven week period; two heats and a Grand National. Could it be that he was falling off the pace?

The Northampton tarmac was another opportunity for the field to assess the effect of the new Hoosier TD. This time John did better but he failed to win the title, partly due to a new innovation pioneered in Britain by Peter Falding. After looking closely at some of the Dutch long track special cars and picking up a few hints from their drivers, Falding was one of a handful of British drivers to experiment with the use of a small block Chevrolet engine in his tarmac car. The smaller engines were lighter, saving about 100kg from the 1300kg big block weight, and allowed drivers to add ballast to the chassis to make the car handle and corner better.

Although John was an innovative racer, particularly in chassis design and tyre choice, he could be a little slow to adapt to new ideas when they were introduced by his opponents rather than from his own workshop. He had been reluctant to adopt an aerofoil roof, introduced by Stuart Smith in the early 1980s, but when he did so in 1986 his performances went through the roof. He was now slow to adapt to small block engines. The reasons were understandable; a new engine would be a considerable financial investment and their reliability was questioned. However, if any driver could afford to fund a new engine through profits earned by racing, surely it was John.

For the moment, small block engines were not a championship-winning breakthrough. Drivers needed time to perfect the weight distribution issues that a small block engine created. Nevertheless, if John had been at the forefront of the small block revolution at this early stage rather than one of the last to join, he may well have continued to command in the mid-nineties with as much domination as he did the late eighties.

Small block Chevrolet aside, the main reason for Falding's success in the European Championship was that he was drawn on the first row of the grid alongside Andy Hodgson and was the clear favourite for the race. He was doubly fortunate because four of his biggest rivals; John, Bert Finnikin, Dave Berresford and Nigel Whorton, were drawn on the back two rows.

So it was no surprise that Falding took the chequered flag first. It was his second title after the World Final in 1986, and some recompense for finishing second in all the major championships in 1989. This time it was John, the man who beat him into second on three of those occasions, who was the runner up. John's drive was magnificent from so far back, but the luck of the draw gave him too much to do. John was third going into the last lap, behind Jayne Bean and in front of Frankie Wainman Junior. Last bend mayhem saw Wainman attack John while John went after Bean. As the three cars tangled and recovered, John crossed the line for second place, Wainman followed for third.

John may have started the season in disappointing fashion, but he still did enough at the qualifying events to start his World Semi-Final at Skegness from pole position. Nigel Whorton started alongside him while Dave Berresford and Bert Finnikin loomed ominously behind on the inside of rows 2 and 3, but it was Kev Smith who threw a spanner in the works. Smith, a regular racer since 1987, had something of a breakthrough season in 1991 and began to finish meeting finals regularly. That gave him a spot on the outside of row 2 in the Skegness World Semi-Final, an unusually high grid position for him. Perhaps he had a touch of nerves and overreacted to it, or perhaps – a little like John in the 1980 World Final – Smith wanted to seize the chance that came his way with both hands. Whatever the reason, Smith launched into the first corner at speed, skittling the cars around him. Nearly all of the front runners were casualties; Whorton and Berresford failed to finish, John lost valuable time extracting himself from the carnage. His car was undamaged and he worked his way back through the field, but only as far as seventh. Finnikin was pleased to survive and take victory, while Smith scraped onto the World Final grid with ninth place, a slipping clutch meaning that he could not hold onto the lead after half distance.

John's annual trip to Baarlo between World Semi-Final and World Final saw him finish the Long Track Championship in second, swapping places with the previous year's runner up, Ron Kroonder. John started on the third row with Peter Falding and early on both Brits made light work of passing Chris Bimmel, Martin Verhoef and Piet Keijzer. Just past half-distance, Falding's chase for first was over when his engine gave up. Were the race held in Britain, John would have had a chance to catch Kroonder because yellow flags were waved while the track was cleared of Falding's oil, but local rules dictated that John had to maintain a long gap behind the leader as the cars rolled round. That cushion allowed Kroonder to cruise to the chequered flag with John back in second, not close enough to challenge on the restart. Third in the Jac Claes Trophy and second in the Hoosier Race topped off John's decent weekend.

Things were less successful at the UK Open Championship at Hartlepool, where John failed to finish the final. Leading the race with a few laps to go, John slowed down and looked to finish safely. He didn't factor for Jayne Bean, who shoved him into the fence as she looked to secure a podium place. Nigel Whorton was left to take an unexpected win.

So John went to the World Championship having lost his British, Long Track and UK Open titles. At least his general form had begun to improve. Spurred along by the imminent World Final, John debuted a new tarmac car at Northampton on 25th August – although it wasn't a completely new car. The previous season's shale car which John had put to one side and made available for sale had not found a new owner. Knowing that the car had been a good runner on tarmac in its first season before it was converted for shale, John decided to recondition it and reconvert it back to tarmac.

John didn't have time to do all the work himself in the middle of a busy season so he sent the car to the workshop of Clive Lintern. It was the first time that John had relinquished control of a chassis, but a fresh pair of eyes helped to discover how the car could be made better. Lintern thought that the back axle needed work and added a coil-over suspension, while Graeme Barr suggested a few ideas for the front. Their advice meant that the car handled better and retained more speed through the corners, something which was immediately obvious at the Northampton final. John nudged ahead of tarmac specialists Chris Elwell and Nigel Whorton with three laps to go; waved yellow flags destroyed any chance of a dramatic last lap response from either opponent. The Northampton win was followed by two others in the month before the World Championship, both on shale, at Bradford and Boston.

Aside from the promising start shown by his new tarmac car, John could also approach the World Final with optimism because the venue, Hednesford, had hosted three major championships in the previous three years and had John won all of them. Moreover, in the timed practice laps run at the start of the World Championship meeting, John was the fastest driver.

Of course, some problems still remained. The biggest was John's loss of advantage in tyre preparation on tarmac. Each of the titles that John had lost over the season had been on a tarmac surface, and Hednesford was the longest tarmac track of all. John had not won any of the four meetings at Hednesford so far in 1991, and only four of his fourteen meeting final wins so far in the season had come on tarmac. And, of course, John's low finish in the World Semi-Final meant that he started the World Final from row 10 of the grid.

Starting a major championship race in the middle of the pack with drivers like John Wright, Russ Humphrey, Phil Smith, New Zealander Barry Podborsky and American Christian Barone around him was an unusual situation for John. The British drivers cumulated ten meeting final victories between them and it was the first World Final appearance for both foreigners. They were all good drivers who had earned their place on merit, but John could not predict how any of them would react when the green flag was waved in a World Final. It was a dangerous position to be in.

John's fears were unfounded and trouble actually broke out at the front of the grid. The two front rowers, Peter Falding and Bert Finnikin, led the field round a very slow rolling lap. The tension made some drivers put their foot to the floor too early and false start, while others stalled. A restart was hastily signalled by the starter, but not before a considerable delay as the drivers of damaged cars rushed to repair them.

In the second and successful start, Falding was knocked wide by Bobby Burns into the path of Finnikin, allowing Andy Hodgson to take the lead ahead of Ron Kroonder. Burns struck again halfway round the first lap, clattering Kroonder into Hodgson, letting Finnikin up the inside. As the first cars roared down the home straight, three drivers had already held the lead in a busy first lap. Finnikin led from Falding, Kroonder, Burns and Hodgson. Burns then forced Kroonder off the racing line, causing him to lose valuable time and allowing numerous cars, including John, to pass. Burns soon retired with tyre damage, having played a key part in a short but incident-packed race.

Back down the grid, John got a good start and immediately pulled away from the drivers around him, working his way through the congested field. Once John caught up with Hodgson he knew that he was in a good position to mount a challenge for the lead. John passed Hodgson round the inside of a turn but didn't get far enough away from him in the straight. Hodgson had to make a split-second decision – to attempt to retake the position or not? He initially went to attack but decided at the last moment to pull back and allow John to go; otherwise he risked John planting him into the fence at the end of the next straight. But in pulling out, Hodgson's bumper knocked John's rear tyre. That affected the handling on John's car slightly, and he eased off from pushing too hard for a few laps in the hope that his damaged tyre would last the distance. John was now rounding the track in third place, the leaders Bert Finnikin and Peter Falding were about a third of a lap in front. Each time John exited a corner he could see Finnikin and Falding going into the next.

Suddenly John saw the starter holding the board signalling that there were five laps remaining. He had missed the Union Jack that indicated the race was at half-distance, and was shocked to find that the race was so close to the finish. John pushed his car to the limit again, knowing that even if his rear tyre suddenly deteriorated he only had to nurse it through a few laps. However, he also knew that he had no real chance to catch the two leaders. All he could do was maintain position and pounce on any opportunity that came his way.

That opportunity arose when Falding attempted a last-bend manoeuvre on Finnikin in a desperate attempt to take the lead at the very end of the race. It had been building for some laps as Falding waited and waited for the right moment. He wanted to pass Finnikin without leaving himself open to attack immediately after, and the last turn was the best moment to do this. Finnikin was expecting the hit and hoped to ride it through the corner. Falding smacked into Finnikin hard, knocking him towards the fence, and Finnikin shredded his outside rear tyre on a stationary car. Falding bounced away from the impact but was then hit by lap-down Richard Pratt and the two cars piled back into Finnikin. John, a few seconds back, had time to ease off the accelerator and take a safe line round the inside of the turn. Kroonder, behind John, was too fast to negotiate the carnage and hit Pratt, knocking the backmarker onto his side. John sailed through to take the chequered flag; Finnikin disentangled himself but was facing backwards. He turned his clumsy three-tyred car and crossed the finish in a cloud of smoke for second place. Falding escaped the melee and limped through for third; Kroonder did the same for fourth. John had been handed the World Championship title in an amazing last few seconds.

Falding was understandably sick that his chance had gone. He had dealt with Finnikin only to be taken out by a backmarker. He did not have much sympathy for Pratt, who suffered four cracked vertebrae from the hits he took on his car. Both contributed to one of the most memorable finishes to a World Final, one that would stay in the memory of all who saw it. Yet in John's opinion it was not his greatest World Final. He realised that he had been lucky, in the right place at the right time.

Still, it felt good to be back under the gold roof. John won five more meetings finals in the run to the end of the season, including the final meeting of the season at Hednesford that hosted the

Grand National Championship. Something of a specialist in that race, John won the Grand National Championship for the sixth season in succession. Not that the gold roof was immune from problems. A spectacular crash occurred at Coventry in October when John smacked into Frankie Wainman Junior side-on. Wainman rolled away while John's front whipped into the air and the car rested momentarily on its back end, pirouetting neatly before the car crashed down heavily on its wheels.

Wainman got revenge when he nicked the Grand Prix Series a month later, his first championship success. John led the series going into the final weekend, when the title would be decided by meetings at Long Eaton and Boston. It looked like he would secure the title with a meeting to spare when he led the meeting final at Long Eaton with a lap to go, but Wainman knocked him into the fence on the last bend to take the win and nip into the series lead. John tried to fight back at Boston, but clipping the wheel of a stationary car in the meeting final caused his retirement and allowed Steve Hodgson and Paul Harrison to sneak in front of him in the series rankings too. After being a quarter of a lap away from clinching the series at Long Eaton, John found himself in fourth.

At least John also had a decent margin of victory in the National Points Championship. He finished with 2775 points; ahead of Peter Falding on 2145 and Frankie Wainman Junior on 1821. Yet the margin of victory disguised a slightly worrying trend. John had won 19 meeting finals over the season, still well clear of Falding's 10 and Wainman's 7; but a drop from John's own 26, 25 and 24 final wins over the previous three seasons. In terms of race wins, the trend was even more worrying. John won 47 races over the season, his lowest return since 1985; both Falding and Wainman won more. John was still the best driver in the sport, but winning races, meeting finals and championships seemed harder that it had been a couple of years before.

1992 started well, perhaps because John did not race in New Zealand for the first time since 1988 and had more hours to devote to the cars in his farm workshop. John won two meeting finals in March and three in April, although it was not enough to stop him sliding to third in the first grading list of the season behind Frankie Wainman Junior and Peter Falding. Three more meeting final wins followed in May, one of which was the UK Open Championship held at Crewe. The big shale oval at Crewe rivalled Hednesford in terms of track length and the wide, open turns meant that drivers tended to power slide right through the corners, their cars sideways and pointing at right angles to the kerb, reminiscent of the old Nelson and Rochdale tracks. This time the title was decided on points accumulated in two heats and a final, and John stormed to victory with a maximum score from wins in both of his heats and the final. He then rounded off the meeting with third in the Grand National. His nearest rival, the veteran Wilf Warnes, finished third and second in his heats and second in the final.

Although the majority of John's success was still coming on shale – all but one of his eight final wins in the first three months were on the loose – he was struggling to fine tune a new addition to a new shale car which had been built over the winter after the old model was sold to brother and sister race team Daniel and Lisa Harter. The new car sported a rear coil-over suspension similar to the Lintern model added to his tarmac car before the World Final in 1991. It gave extra stability and speed, but getting the suspension right in race conditions was a slow process of experimentation. Once it proved itself at Crewe, the most uneven shale track, John knew he was nearly there.

The weekend before the UK Open John travelled to Hednesford for the European Championship. The grid was based on British and Dutch grading lists, with the top scorers at the front, so John's slip to third place was untimely. He started on the inside of row 3, with Frankie Wainman Junior and Ron Kroonder on the front row and Chris Bimmel and Peter Falding on the second row.

The front rowers hesitated at the start. Falding ineffectually used his bumper on Kroonder to try and get past, Bimmel was more successful and went into the lead by snaking past Wainman, although he lost it to a recovering Wainman on the second lap. John made his way past Falding, who was using his shale car and struggling to keep up with the leaders, and Bimmel, who also seemed to lack speed. Once John had edged past Kroonder, only Wainman remained between him and the championship.

By halfway through the race, Wainman still held a lead over John, who was increasingly concerned that the drying track would benefit Wainman more than himself. That spurred John into an early overtaking manoeuvre; he applied the accelerator and launched into the leader. Since he had to make up a few metres down the straight before hitting Wainman, John carried too much speed into the corner and followed him wide. Wainman hit a stationary car and stalled, allowing John to yank his car back to the inside line and into the lead. He motored down the home straight ahead of Kroonder, Falding and Harrison. Wainman restarted his engine and rejoined the race, now a lap down and just behind John. Looking for payback, he clattered John into Will Yarrow. John managed to control the impact and got back on the racing line. Kroonder had a chance to make up some of the distance to the leader but could not get close enough for last lap heroics, John kept a safe distance between them to the chequered flag. John's remarkable run of championship success at

Hednesford continued; his fifth win in five major championship meetings there since 1987. Wainman was left licking his wounds.

The top drivers met up again for the British Championship at Coventry on 6th June. John finished his heats in eleventh and sixth which left him in a poor grid position on row 10, but John was not alone among the top drivers. With the exception of Dave Berresford, the heats were won by less well-known drivers: Shane Dorrell won two, Richard Mason and Graham France each won one. Peter Falding managed two fourth places, Bert Finnikin finished fourth and eleventh, Frankie Wainman Junior was fourth and seventh. Business as usual returned in the final, however, as the better drivers pushed their way through. The inexperienced front rowers cracked under the pressure and Dorrell, Mason and France did not finish in the top ten. John edged past those in front of him to third place, where he nestled in behind Bobby Burns. He nearly got into second too, sneaking inside Burns round a turn, when an unexpected attack from Wainman clattered both John and Burns into the fence. Wainman went on to finish first and take his first championship title, cheerfully admitting that John 'did me in the European so I did him in this one'. John recovered from the Wainman hit but was far from victory in eighth.

John won a solitary meeting final victory in June, at Hartlepool the day after the British Championship. Although that may seem like little success, he put together a run of eight consecutive second or third places in meeting finals that took him into July. Two more final victories followed, at Long Eaton and Skegness.

John's World Championship campaign took him to pole position in the World Semi-Final at Hartlepool. Failing to spot the starter wave the green flag, John allowed fellow front-rower Frankie Wainman Junior to surge ahead down the home straight. John retained second for a few laps before claiming the lead when Wainman hooked his bumper onto that of a backmarker. A couple of circuits later, John lost the lead when traffic slowed him. Wainman stayed in first place after the race was temporarily stopped by waved yellow flags, but the stoppage allowed John to close the gap and he was now looking for an opportunity to pass. That arose when John Wright skidded across the track and was hit side-on, pushing him into a rollover just as the leaders approached. Wainman passed the upended car on the outside line, while John kept his foot on the accelerator and went on the inside. Yellow flags were waved a second time to deal with Wright's car, but not before John had sneaked into first place. He made sure that he kept a gap at the restart and maintained it until the end, Wainman followed him in second with Bobby Burns third.

A strong clutch of drivers had made their way through to the front rows of the World Final grid, but the top places in the other World Semi-Final were claimed by less obvious candidates. Nigel Whorton failed to start the race, while Peter Falding and Bert Finnikin failed to finish. Jayne Bean, the sport's best female driver who started from the front row, also failed to finish. It was Danny Clarke, Dave Berresford and Russ Humphrey who took advantage of others' misfortune to claim the right to start alongside John, Wainman and Burns on the front three rows of the World Final.

As usual, John nipped off to Holland before the World Final. The Long Track Championship always required John's tarmac car to be altered for the long straights and higher speed, but this time the intricacies of the setup were even more difficult with the addition of heavy rain. The puddles got so bad that John initially swapped his outside wheels from Hoosier slicks to Dirt Stockers, usually a shale tyre, but he swapped back to Hoosier treaded tyres just before the grid formed. With rain still falling, Falding and John lined up on row 3, behind Piet Keijzer, Ron Kroonder, Martin Verhoef and Chris Bimmel.

The top six made it through the first two laps safely. The corners were the best place for grip as the steep banks drained the water to the centre green, the main problem was on the long straights where standing water meant that aquaplaning was a real possibility. The tricky conditions first claimed Bimmel, who got a corner wrong on lap 3 and lost so much speed that he was relegated fourteen places. Verhoef followed him next time round, drifting into the fence on the exit of the last turn. Two laps later, Kroonder lost control and recovered only when most of the field had passed him.

Keijzer was now out in front, pursued by Falding and John. Falding found his way through on lap 7, while John had to wait until lap 16. By that time Falding had got up enough of a lead that John was never in contention. Falding passed the chequered flag to claim his third Long Track Championship, while John was runner up for the second year in a row. Chris Elwell completed an all-British podium with a good drive from row 11.

Attention now turned back to the World Final at Bradford. John did not repeat his mistake of two years before, when he raced the same car on the punishing Baarlo tarmac and Bradford shale without checking that the car was in good order in between. This time, John thought that his shale car was good enough for the World Final. There would be no risk of a misfiring tarmac engine ruining his chances.

John went to the World Championship meeting in a good run of form, hoping to repeat his double World Final victories of 1987 and 1988. Apart from the Long Track Championship meeting, John accrued three British meeting final wins in the six week gap between World Semi-Final and World Final, along with two second places, two thirds and two fourths.

John's driving style on the Bradford shale was similar to that which he employed on the Hednesford tarmac. The gradient and width of the corners meant that he could go into them at speed, drifting out wide to the fence, a racing line which meant that he could hammer the accelerator down as he exited the corner onto the straight. It had worked in three out of six meeting finals so far at Bradford, and John hoped that it would continue to do so at the most important race of the season. Moreover, his new rear coil-over suspension was now proving to be a good investment, giving John extra speed over the shale lumps and bumps.

Danny Clarke won the toss of the coin between the two World Semi-Final winners, meaning that he started on pole with John alongside him on the outside of the front row. Frankie Wainman Junior and Dave Berresford started on row 2. Most observers thought that the 1992 World Champion was likely to come from the front two rows. Bert Finnikin and Peter Falding had failed to finish both their World Semi-Final and the Consolation Semi-Final, although Falding had crept onto the back of the grid by virtue of a technicality. Since winning the Long Track Championship three weeks before, Falding claimed the right to start on the grid by virtue of being a World Champion: the Long Track World Champion. It was stretching the regulations to the limit; the rule was designed to allow the reigning short track champion to defend his title, and the officials and Falding both knew it. However, he was allowed to start the race, although he was surely too far back to be anything else apart from another backmarker to pass.

The Bradford shale was wet and there were plenty of cars sliding and struggling for grip on the slow rolling lap. John kept level with Clarke as they edged round the last turn before the green flag and tried to hold his line. The Bradford corners were steeply cambered, and as John entered the corner his car slipped down the shale and impacted with Clarke, a side-on-side collision. It was nothing too severe, but the knock shifted Clarke's direction slightly. John roared away as he exited the turn into the home straight and under the green flag; Clarke twitched sideways, holding up many of the cars behind him. Berresford followed John round the outside line and into second place.

Other drivers were struggling for control and many tangled on the first turn, blocking part of the track. This was exactly the type of situation that could damage John's title prospects; he could get tangled up in the melee and lose time, he could take damage to his car, or he could be taken out by another car trying to avoid or escape the mess. Trying to stay well clear of everybody else, John took a high line through the corner but lost traction as his tyres slipped on the loose shale at the top of the bank. He slid into the fence but was lucky that the impact was side-on, just as he had swiped Clarke on the opening bend. The energy did not buckle John's wheels or axles and he suffered no damage. By the time he had completed another lap of the track, the melee had been cleared and John could find a safe line without needing to go so high.

It was his biggest scare of the race. Safely through the pile-up, John and Berresford were quickly up with the backmarkers and working their way through traffic. John scythed his way through the pack, picking up more of a lead after Berresford retired on lap 8. By the time he passed the chequered flag he was half a lap in front of Bobby Burns. John had survived unscathed in a disjointed and unpredictable race. He seemed to calmly and serenely continue on as those around him were slowed or held up by events on the track, the sure sign of a driver in full control of his car and the race situation. In an illustration of how many other drivers suffered in the tricky conditions, Falding came from row 18 for third place and Rob Cowley drove to fourth from row 14.

John's fourth World Championship success elevated him to another level in the sport. He was a double World Champion for the second time and only Stuart Smith had worn the gold roof more often. Few could argue against the statistics and the claim that John was the second best driver in the history of the sport, eclipsing such names as Johnny Brise, Dave Chisholm, Willie Harrison, Fred Mitchell and Frankie Wainman.

In a comfortable run to the end of the season John won two more meeting finals, at Crewe and Hartlepool, the second of which was the penultimate round of the Grand Prix Series. The series was five rounds old before the World Championship meeting and there were now eight left to run. John did not win a final until the Hartlepool meeting, but his consistent finishes of two second places, four thirds and two fourths meant that John won the series with 395 points, ahead of Paul Harrison on 364 and Frankie Wainman Junior on 349. All that remained was the Grand National Championship, held at Scunthorpe on 21st November. John hoped to make it seven consecutive wins, but he was to be disappointed. Kev Smith managed to scrape home in first place and John had to settle for second.

At least John could maintain his run of consecutive titles in the National Points Championship. The final table had a similar look to the previous season. John won the marathon comfortably with 2919, a lead of 739 points over Frankie Wainman Junior in second, while Peter Falding was third with 1994. Just like the previous year, John had won fewer races over the season than Wainman and Falding, but he held it together in meetings finals, winning 17 compared to Wainman's 15 and Falding's 8.

It was John's sixth consecutive National Points Championship. Although it paled in comparison to Stuart Smith's thirteen consecutive titles between 1969 and 1982, it was still far ahead of any other driver's achievements. The next closest were Frankie Wainman, who won three consecutive National Points Championships before John won his first in 1987, and Fred Mitchell, who won three in a four year period in between 1957 and 1960. John's silver roof – or silver stripes in the four years that he wore gold too – signified that he was the most consistently successful driver on the track.

The silver roof actually meant little to John. He went out to win races, finals and championships, not to build up a stockpile of grading points. However, one inevitably follows the other, and nobody could argue that John was the most successful driver in the six years that he was the National Points Champion.

Yet another success

9

End of an Era
1993-94

The 1993 season started late and drivers did not get on track to unveil their new cars until 1ˢᵗ May at Coventry. The delay also caused a reduction in the number of race meetings from 91 in 1992 to 66 in 1993, and although the schedule would return to a late March start in subsequent years the number of meetings would never recover. Fewer meetings meant that drivers were able to race at a higher proportion rather than picking and choosing which they attended and helped to level the playing field in the grading list.

As always, the technological and mechanical race continued. The move towards small block engines had continued in 1992; Murray Harrison built a small block car and Frankie Wainman Junior went for radical small block power in his shale car. Peter

Falding followed Wainman's lead and introduced a small block shale car for the new season. Big block engines would soon become a disadvantage, especially on tarmac, but John decided that he would continue to use them since he had two perfectly good big block Chevrolets. To counter the small blocks he changed the engine casing on his tarmac car to an aluminium one. By encasing it in a lighter metal he saved a bit of weight and made the car more competitive. It was not enough to claw back the advantage that drivers with small block engines had, but it did narrow the gap.

On shale, John was behind the wheel of another new car. For the second time in two seasons Daniel and Lisa Harter purchased John's shale car at the end of the season. This time the 1991 car was part-exchanged back to John in return for his 1992 car. The old car was stored on the farm, slowly rusting, waiting to see if it would get another chance on track, while John hoped that his new 1993 shale model would benefit from the experience he had gained building the two older ones.

John's first meeting final victory came at Long Eaton. It was a filthy, grotty day, so bad that Murray Harrison's goggles became caked in mud and visibility was so poor that he slammed into the fence. He was stretchered from the track with career-threatening injuries; a broken collarbone and two cracked vertebrae, but was back on track within a few months. Two other periods of waved yellows in the race condensed the field, each of which allowed John to close the distance to the front runners and take the lead. 35 minutes after the race started the chequered flag was finally waved as John crossed the line.

Two weeks later John returned to Long Eaton for the British Championship. There he finished one heat only, in third place. That left him too far back on the championship grid to make much impression and he failed to finish the race. John retired early, as did Frankie Wainman Junior, who also had a poor meeting. In the European Championship race John finished fifth, too far away to challenge Peter Falding.

It was a similar disappointing story at Baarlo in the Long Track Championship. Initially it looked like John might challenge for the title. A first turn pile-up caught out many of the fancied Dutch drivers, while defending champion Peter Falding lost control of an unfamiliar borrowed car and spun on the first lap. That left John in second, behind Ron Kroonder and in front of Henk Jan Ronitz, but the race was halted for a full restart after two more laps when marshals decided that Piet Keijzer needed attention in his stationary car. On the restart, only Kroonder and John were able to grid from the first six cars. Kroonder kept clear when the green flag fell for a second time while John battled to keep up. By lap 13, four from the end, he retired to the centre green with a flat tyre. The first six finishers were all Dutch; the host nation had emphatically seized back the Long Track Championship after a period of British domination. John's hard time continued; tenth place in the Jac Claes Trophy was his only race finish of the weekend.

Only fifteen drivers went north to Hartlepool for the UK Open Championship, a meeting which was dominated by a familiar surname. Andy Smith, son of Stuart, won two heats and the final and was a clear leader in the accumulated points. It was Smith's first championship in his first full season of racing and the emphatic way that he won the title meant that it was not just because of his famous father that he was one to watch in the future. John was still in the hunt before the final, second in the standings, but fifth place in the final dropped him just short of the podium.

The late start to the season meant that the eight World Championship qualifying meetings were crammed into a short four week period from mid-May to mid-June. John won the Long Eaton meeting final and took two other podiums to give him a front row spot in the World Semi-Final at Buxton. His biggest rival on the grid, Frankie Wainman Junior, started alongside. Both roared away at the green flag, but an error on lap 2 relegated John to fourth behind Ian Platts and Jamie Davidson. He made up for his mistake by passing Platts and Davidson by quarter-distance. Halfway through the race a broken drive shaft ended Wainman's race and gave John the lead. He stayed there until the finish, Platts and Davidson got on the podium and secured good positions on the World Final grid. In the other World Semi-Final at Skegness, which boasted more of the top drivers, there were no surprises: Peter Falding won, followed by Nigel Whorton, Paul Harrison and Bert Finnikin.

The World Final at Coventry on 4th September was John's second chance to win three World Finals on the bounce and he was starting from the front row. The odds were far more favourable this time. In 1989 John started from the back of the World Final grid, this time he was right at the front. But it was not to be.

Peter Falding won the coin toss for pole position and got off to a good start, taking a fast line through the first bend. John squeezed in behind him and the two front rowers opened up a small gap from the chasing pack. Five laps in, Rick Standridge left his front axle on a fence post and John Lawn played dodgems with the fence at the other end of the track. A 30 minute race suspension gave drivers the chance to leap out of the cab and check their cars.

On the restart John looked for a chance to get past Falding, but they both circled the track without swapping position. After eight laps, John was close enough to nudge Falding's back bumper, but the leader was unmoved. Spectators were expecting John to hold on and wait for a last bend attack, just as Falding waited to hit Bert Finnikin in the riotous finish in 1991. John had other ideas and decided to move much earlier. He launched into Falding with just nine laps gone, but John didn't manage to hit perfectly square and he lost control of his car, sliding sideways into Warren Hunter. Nigel Whorton sneaked into the lead, Falding kept going after taking a wide line round the bend and rejoined in second while John continued to chase from third. Within a lap, however, he turned onto the centre green, the impact with Hunter having caused a flat tyre. Falding was left to overtake Whorton, who held the lead for only a lap, then deal with Ian Platts, who also caught the front runners. Having seen off all challengers, Falding completed an easy second half of the race for his second World Final win.

Everybody expressed an opinion afterwards and the common consensus was that John had tried to pass Falding too early. Why didn't he hang on until the last lap? It looked like impatience had cost John his crown.

He did have his reasons. Not long before the World Final, Dunlop introduced a new shale tyre which Falding had opted to use on his rear outside wheel. John stuck with Hoosiers, the tyre he found to be more reliable. The different tyres meant that John thought his car outperformed Falding's at the start, but Falding's defensive driving was first-class and John could not find a route past. When the race was suspended it was clear that the shale was drying out and the loose stuff was being shifted from the racing line. The changing conditions meant that Falding's Dunlop improved while John's Hoosier found less speed and grip. John thought that if he didn't get past Falding quickly he would soon be left behind, not close enough to attempt a big hit on the last lap. Although the early attack did not work out and John was forced to retire, at least he knew that he had made the attempt instead of meekly letting his rival drive away from him.

So the chance for three in a row was lost a second time. A further slap in the face came when John was barred from racing in the meeting consolation because 30 cars had already taken to the grid. The officials blindly ignored the fact that John's transporter was at the far end of the crowded pits and he had to negotiate his way there and back between the end of the World Final and start of the consolation. Parked up on the wrong side of the safety fence as the consolation got under way, John got nothing out of the World Championship meeting.

Some compensation arrived in the form of the Grand Prix Series. Although he did not win any of the nine rounds, John's meeting final results of two seconds, a third and three fourths was enough to give him the title. Going into the final round at Stoke, John had a slender six-point lead over Frankie Wainman Junior. The last meeting decider was a near wash-out and mechanical problems meant that Wainman failed to score. Finishes of second, fifth and sixth in John's three races were enough to send the trophy home with him.

First he lost the gold roof, next he lost the silver. John's lack of meeting final victories was not just a phenomenon in the Grand Prix Series. Over the whole season he won only two meeting finals, at Long Eaton and Bradford. He won only 21 races in total, less than half the amount of the previous year, and a fifth of his best season total of 101 in 1988. The drop in the number of race meetings in the calendar was not enough to disguise the fact that John's race results had deteriorated. He no longer had the consistent form necessary to top the grading list and slipped back to third place at the end of the season. The new National Points Champion was the same driver who had stolen the World Championship title, Peter Falding, who won with 1872 points and eleven final wins, an increase on his figures from the previous year despite the drop in the number of meetings. Frankie Wainman

Junior claimed 1581 points, John was third with 1491. For the first time since 1987 John would start a season under a red roof.

John had lost a little motivation and interest, although he still raced in 60 meetings, more than any other driver. To some extent he was going through the motions towards the end of the season, aware that he had lost the gold roof and would soon lose the silver one. Yet to say that John lost the titles rather than Falding won them is grossly unfair. John's dip coincided with Falding's best season, and he finished 1993 as European, National Points and World Champion. It was an excellent return for Falding, who had been John's major rival over the previous six years. John's preeminent status in the sport was being seriously challenged. Falding had the potential to rule over stock car racing in the mid-nineties just as successfully as John had done in the late-eighties.

Domestic upheaval must also bear some of the responsibility for John's loss of form. After ten years of marriage, John and Sarah separated in September. It was a shock to John. Sarah moved away from the farm with 8 year-old James and 5 year-old Sam, finding a home in nearby Gisburn. Although they remained on friendly terms and both sons were able to see both their parents, the strain of John's second marriage breakdown was far harder than the first because children were involved.

Looking to recharge his batteries, get away from the farm and rediscover his enthusiasm for racing, John returned to New Zealand in the off-season at the invitation of Spike Richardson. Driving a car loaned from Bryce Penn, John managed three race finishes at the 240 Championship, in fifteenth, fourteenth and thirteenth, leaving him eleventh in the final standings. It was not his finest performance in New Zealand, but he was still first among the British entrants: Paul Harrison was sixteenth, Peter Falding twentieth and Formula 2 driver Len Perkins did not score.

In something a little different, John took to the grid a week later as the captain of the Rest of the World in a team race against five New Zealanders. John lined up with Harrison, Falding, Australian Glen Battersby and New Zealander Frank van vroon Hoven. The rules were simple – from a clutch start, the winning team was the one represented by the first car over the line at the end of the race. It was more akin to banger racing than true stock car racing. John tangled straight away with Paul Demanser, the New Zealand captain, but fought back to third place by the end. Roydon Collingwood held the lead for the majority of the race and by the last lap John was left resorting to desperate measures, parking up on the final turn, hoping to take out Collingwood. The New Zealanders were too canny to fall foul of the obvious obstruction and Demanser blocked John, allowing Collingwood through for the win.

Such brazen tactics were not allowed back in the UK, so if John were to see off Peter Falding's challenge to his supremacy back on the regular British tracks he needed to go back to basics and find the form that took him to so many victories in the late-eighties. Moreover, he would have to overcome a new problem. Over the winter a BSCDA meeting banned aluminium engine blocks. That did not matter to drivers with small block Chevrolets who already had a weight advantage; it was big block drivers who would need to find a new way to get competitive. Chris Elwell complained that his aluminium engine block would take time to replace and was given a few months dispensation to make the change. At the same meeting that Elwell spoke out, John kept quiet. He had built a new tarmac car which retained an aluminium engine block but did not declare it. It meant that he received no dispensation and was running an illegal tarmac car.

John's results on tarmac the previous year with his aluminium-cased big block Chevrolet had not been noteworthy. Since he was gaining no competitive advantage by sticking with his old engine, he thought that there would be little need to scrutinise his setup. John intended to shift to an alternative at some point in the future, but did not want to be tied down to making an expensive small block purchase in a matter of weeks, as Elwell would have to if he wanted to remain competitive.

Whatever the reason, it was a deliberate snub of the rules. John hoped to keep his head down and avoid drawing attention to his car. His ploy was dashed when officials did a round of the Northampton pits a week before the British Championship with magnets in hand, checking that they stuck to the steel engine casings. John held his breath as the scrutineers poked around under his bonnet, mentally composing excuses in his head. Yet surprisingly the scrutineers surfaced and declared the car fit to race. John did not know where they had put the magnets, but they must have stuck to something. Realising he just had a lucky escape, John gathered his team at the workshop and they swapped the aluminium engine plate for a steel one. It would harm his chances at the British Championship, but John realised that he could not hope to be so lucky a second time.

As it turns out, John did not need to fit his new engine casing so quickly. He was not destined to race at the British Championship at all. The transporter bus ground to a halt on the M62 with a seized wheel bearing. Luckily the bus expired by a phonebox and John managed to call the farm to ask for a replacement to be driven out to them. While they waited, John tried to remove the wheel but it would not budge. Luckily a former driver, Rodney Mitchell, happened to go past on his way home from work. He stopped to help and the wheel was eventually removed, but not until Mitchell sourced a spanner and welded pieces of metal to it at his workshop so it would fit the wheel nut. By the time the bus was repaired it was too late to make the meeting. John continued on to Skegness since there was a Sunday race meeting too, but the chance to win the British Championship was gone.

Shifting to a steel engine casing did not stop rumours spreading on the pit grapevine that John had been racing for two months with an illegal setup. Some thought that he was using a metal-based paint to get through scrutineering. Ian Higgins, Chairman of the BSCDA, rang John to ask him directly whether he had been using an aluminium engine casing. John evaded the question like a skilful Westminster politician, telling Higgins that he was free to check underneath his bonnet at the next meeting.

There were some calls for John to be stripped of all the grading and World Championship qualifying points he had accumulated over the first few weeks of the season. That would have severely dented his chances in the National Points Championship and demoted him down the grid for the World Semi-Final. It could even have been enough to drop out of superstar grade if he could not make up enough points in the next couple of months. It would have been a draconian punishment, but John stood firm. There was no proof beyond rumours that he had raced with an aluminium engine casing, so there was no case against him. He retained the points he had won so far, but he was now cornered and had no option but to race with a steel engine casing. That undoubtedly affected his race performance for the rest of the season.

Not that his results were outstanding beforehand. At the first new grading list of the season John found himself in seventh place with only one race victory, a heat at Bradford. Above him were Danny Clarke, Dave Berresford, Steve Hodgson, Paul Harrison, Peter Falding and Frankie Wainman Junior. By the next grading list, based on results up to 20th May, John had worked his way back up to third behind Wainman and Falding, but still with only three race wins.

John went into the European Championship at Northampton, eleven weeks into the season, having failed to win a single meeting final. Even worse, he failed to finish in nine out of the 22 finals that he raced in. Peter Falding, by contrast, had won three and Frankie Wainman Junior had won five. The European Championship, however, saw a small upturn in John's fortunes.

The grid was decided by a random draw, and again John was not one of the lucky ones – when the promoters decided to set the European grid in this way, John always seemed to get a bad draw. Peter Falding and Ron Kroonder had the benefit of starting near the front, John was left languishing at the back. Falding took advantage of his good fortune and retained the title, Kroonder was second; but John won the most praise by working his way through the field for third place. He followed up the podium position with a win in the next race, heat 1 of the race meeting, his sixth race win of the season, and second in the meeting final. The first championship meeting of the season was not a fairy tale story of success, but it was something of a turning point.

Seven days later John was one of few drivers who bothered to travel up to Hartlepool for the UK Open Championship. The north-eastern track, the last remaining in the area, was in its death throes and struggling to attract more than twenty cars to meetings. Following the UK Open it would host just four more meetings over the next two and a half seasons before it was dropped from the schedule, largely unmourned. Only fourteen drivers arrived on this occasion, of whom John and Frankie Wainman Junior were the big names, with Andy Smith, Kev Smith and Frankie Wainman Senior bulking out the back of the grid. John knew that it was likely that there would be few cars and an open track to race on so he used the meeting to test a new setup, borrowing a small block Chevrolet and putting it in his tarmac car.

Steve Hodgson won heat 1 and came second in heat 2 to put himself in a strong position for the championship. Andy Smith was in the best position to challenge him with second and third place in the heats, while Richard Mason won a heat and had a fourth in the other. Both Wainmans finished down the order and looked out of the running. John had a third and a fifth, nothing too spectacular, but he was quickly learning how the small block engine affected his handling and the best way to adjust his car to get the maximum benefit from the reduced weight.

The meeting final offered double points, so there were still five or six drivers in with a realistic chance of winning. John took the chequered flag first, but the overall title depended on where the others finished. Frankie Wainman Junior finished second; Hodgson was third, giving the same amount of points as John. Ties were decided by who had the better place in the final, so the title went to John. Had Hodgson squeezed into second place, the UK Open title would have been his. It was John's first final win of the season, and it was on tarmac. After the meeting, John was spotted near his open bonnet, looking thoughtfully at the small block Chevrolet, tape measure in hand. Would the next tarmac car from the Lund workshop have small block power? Despite his victory, John was still unconvinced. His big block engine was now five years old, whereas many of the small block engines struggled to survive a full season.

John hoped for more tarmac success at Baarlo in the Long Track Championship, especially since he could refit the aluminium engine casing which complied with Dutch regulations. Starting from the sixth row, John made his way past Henk Jan Ronitz, Sjaak Valk and Hennie Cuppens by the end of the long first lap. His high point was seventh, after which he dropped back to eighth at the chequered flag. Ron Kroonder seemed to have perfected long track racing and took his second consecutive title. John was happier in the Jac Claes Trophy, where he finished third, and the meeting final, where he improved one place to second. However, although he was mostly on the pace at Baarlo, as soon as he returned to Britain his aluminium engine casing was switched back to steel. The weight problems associated with John's heavy big block engine were yet to be overcome.

That wasn't an issue for the World Championships. In 1993 the highest qualifying points scorer was given a choice of World Semi-Final venue rather than selecting randomly by a coin toss. Frankie Wainman Junior chose the Stoke tarmac, which meant that as the second highest qualifying points scorer, John was sent to the Long Eaton World Semi-Final to race on shale. That suited John fine, it was the race he would have chosen anyway. And since the World Final was scheduled for Bradford, John would not require his tarmac car in his challenge for the gold roof.

The trouble was that John failed to finish the race at Long Eaton, despite starting from pole on his preferred surface. Paul Harrison found the most traction at the start and took an early lead. On the fourth lap, Harrison hesitated behind backmarkers and John nipped through into the lead. That should have been it, normal service resumed, until two laps later when a number of cars tangled on the home straight. John went to the outside to avoid them and caught his tyre on the fence. It quickly deflated and John was forced onto the centre green, out of the race. Kev Smith took victory, followed by Harrison and Rob Cowley. Since he was not the reigning champion, John could not claim a place on the World Final grid unless he finished in the top two of the Consolation Semi-Final.

That race was swiftly arranged at Coventry after the intended venue, the short-lived Bolton track, closed suddenly in August. It was another blow to the sport in the north; Bolton was added to a growing scrap heap which also included Crewe and Boston, both of which hosted their last meetings at the end of 1993. At least the move from Bolton to Coventry meant that the Consolation Semi-Final was also on shale. Most of the other big names had made their way through already, so John lined up at the back of the grid as the strong favourite to progress. He did so, although not in first place. Gaz Bott won, John finished second with a damaged front suspension, Les Spencer just missed out on the World Final in third having held off John until the last few laps.

John knew that he stood little chance in the World Final, even though Bradford's big shale bowl was one of his favourite tracks. Starting at the very back of the grid, he would have to make his way past all 29 opponents to win. Sitting pretty on pole position was Dave Berresford, who now raced less and tended to pick the meetings that would help him to win the elusive World Championship title. Now that Bert Finnikin had retired, Berresford was one of the few racers who survived from the early and mid-seventies, along with Frankie Wainman, Danny Clarke, Bobby Burns and John; but John was the only one who still raced with the same dedication as he did in his early years. Alongside Berresford was Kev Smith, his best grid position in a World Final, while three of the bright young things; Paul Harrison, Andy Smith and Frankie Wainman Junior, started just behind.

Berresford did his best to hold back the tide of change, but could not prevent Frankie Wainman Junior and Andy Smith getting through. Wainman retired when his cooling system failed; Smith went on to win the World Final, a shock result considering his age and inexperience, but another sign that he was destined for future greatness. Yet it could have been so different. Barring mechanical failure, John could have actually done the unbelievable and come right through the field to take the win. Had it happened, it would have surely gone down as the most remarkable drive in stock car history. John's car was flying and he worked his way through the field with his usual Bradford technique of pushing his car deep and fast into the corners and hammering the accelerator down as quickly as possible on the exit. By half-distance John was in eighth place and still passing opponents. It was all going so well until his clutch started to slip. He lost power slightly, and ceased gaining on the front runners at the rate he had done earlier in the race, even dropping back a place on the final lap.

Andy Smith won, Kev Smith was second, Berresford third. Then Rob Cowley and Richard Mason finished, and John followed them in sixth. It was still a great performance from the back of the grid, but John was frustrated and felt that he could have made the podium, even the top step, had his engine not faltered. As the cars pulled to a halt and waited for the pit gate to open, John's car seized up. The bell housing was red hot.

In the six-week drift to the end of the season John won two meeting finals, one each at Hartlepool and Northampton. The Hartlepool meeting earned John the BSCDA Bumper Trophy, while the Northampton meeting also featured the Grand National Championship, which John reclaimed after two years. Those meeting final wins increased John's total for the season to five; he won 26 races in total during the season. Both were an improvement on the previous year but were not enough to redeem the National Points Championship. The same three drivers shared the top spots as they had for the last four years, but the order shifted again. Frankie Wainman Junior squeezed home first in a tight race with Peter Falding, 1672 points to 1624. John was a close third with 1531.

It was now two years since John had won the World Final. The last time that had happened, in 1989 and 1990, he still won two National Points titles, two British Championships and one European Championship. This time he had gone two years without a single major championship trophy. Perhaps the Lund era was over?

Heading the grid in the 1995 World Final

10

Under Pressure
1995

The pressure was slowly building. John needed to be back on the top step of the podium if he were to remain other drivers' most feared and respected opponent. The first chance to do that was when he returned to the other side of the world to compete for the one trophy that had eluded him in his career.

John's lack of success in the 240 Championship was not surprising since he had to race in a borrowed car and could not make full use of his years of experience in car setup. This time he was in one belonging to Murray Long.

Spike Richardson had changed the format slightly. Drivers still raced in three heats as before, but only to accumulate points to decide a grid for the final on which the 240 Championship title depended. It meant that the New Zealanders were unusually timid in the heats, saving their cars for the big race. John made a primitive error in the first heat and ran out of fuel. In the second he battled his way from the back to finish eighth, while in the third he recovered well from riding the wall, his outside wheels high on the fence and his inside wheels on the track, to finish tenth.

That put John on the eighth row in the championship race, two rows ahead of Andy Smith but behind Paul Harrison, Peter Falding and Frankie Wainman Junior. None of the Brits did well in the key race; Falding was the highest finisher in eighth while John was way back having been caught up in a mid-grid pile-up. The New Zealanders kept the title in their own country but were unhappy with the new format of the new championship, feeling that the qualification process for the final encouraged tame and monotonous driving in the heats.

Hard-driving and plenty of bumper was the Kiwi way, something best illustrated in team races. In the first of two New Zealand v Rest of the World challenge races, John took to the track alongside three teammates from last year; Harrison, Falding, and Australian Glen Battersby, together with New Zealander Barry Podborsky. Starting from pole, John allowed Lyall Rumney into the lead but was taken out when Rumney waited for him on the far straight and plastered him against the wall. The brutal tactics missing from the 240 Championship were back. Rumney recovered to take the win for New Zealand, John was out with a puncture. John started the second race on pole again. This time he worked with Falding to take fellow front rower Roydon Collingwood into the wall. Rumney went into the lead again, holding it to the end of the race, despite John and Harrison working together to ambush him on the last lap.

The New Zealanders might have thought that tactics and race craft employed in the new-style 240 Championship was tame, but it was the style of racing that John excelled at. The British season started with some consistent top-five heat and final finishes. A meeting final victory at Stoke came courtesy of some last bend fireworks between John, Frankie Wainman Junior and Paul Harrison. Each was in with a chance of winning, but John crawled over the line first, just in front of Harrison and Wainman.

The Stoke final apart, Frankie Wainman Junior was out of the blocks quickly, winning six of the first eleven meetings. Nevertheless, in the first grading list of the season Paul Harrison sat at the top, Wainman was second and John third. Peter Falding was seventh, dropping down after combining stock car racing with Eurocars, a new non-contact Ford Mondeo based saloon formula. Lower-grade drivers got on the top step of the podium in May with eight different drivers winning the eight race meetings, none of whom were John, Harrison, Wainman or Falding.

The first major event of the season was the European Championship held at Northampton over a full weekend towards the end of May. John was consistent, finishing each of the seven races in which he took part, but the championship race was his worst result: ninth. Frankie Wainman Junior headed a strong podium that included Andy Smith and Peter Falding.

Two weekends later the British Championship was hosted by Coventry. No driver dominated the heats on a wet track, which meant that John's results of second, fifth and fourth gave him pole position in the championship race. Paul Harrison, with two thirds and a fifth, was next to him. Neither Andy Smith nor Frankie Wainman Junior scored highly and Peter Falding was absent, so it looked like Harrison would be John's major competition.

After two restarts the cars finally got away for a much-delayed championship race at 11pm. John took the lead and Harrison fell back. Berresford made his way to third from row 3 of the grid and Frankie Wainman Junior charged to fourth from row 5.

Wainman continued past Berresford but found Harrison harder to pass. Wainman's frustration made him attack too heavily; both he and Harrison hit the fence and sustained punctures, second and third placed drivers retiring together. John went through to take the chequered flag without challenge, followed by Dave Berresford and Andy Smith. It was John's first major championship since the National Points title in 1992. The pressure on John's shoulders was relieved slightly; he had proven that he was not over the hill just yet.

On his next visit to Coventry, John left in a far different mood – as did everybody associated with the sport. It was all going well in the meeting final until John raced onto the home straight at the head of a pack of cars that included Paul Harrison, Rob Cowley, John Cayzer and Frankie Wainman Junior. Lying at a right angle across the home straight was the car of John Goodhall, who lost control after clipping the fence. John twitched to one side, but those following him were unsighted. Wainman's front bumper hit Goodhall side-on. The impact caused Goodhall to immediately lose consciousness and the race was quickly stopped. Within an hour or so Goodhall succumbed to his injuries, a fractured neck and skull. Safety had much improved since John first started racing nearly two decades before, but it was impossible to remove the risk of full-contact motorsport completely. Goodhall was a tragic victim of a racing incident.

John's UK Open Championship title was lost to Paul Harrison after he finished the final in fourth place. The loss of a minor championship was a setback, but the best way that John could prove he was a continuing threat was to win back the World Championship crown. All seemed to be in order at the World Semi-Final at Skegness, where John started from pole position. He led into the first corner, but Will Yarrow crashed and spilled oil on the track so a restart was ordered. John repeated his strong start, but this time fellow front rower Paul Harrison slipped back into third and Jamie Davidson sneaked into second. Each seemed happy with their slot, and the race turned into a merry-go-round without incident. John would start the World Final from the front row.

Then the Long Track Championship interrupted the season again. John started the main championship race from sixth on the grid; both he and Frankie Wainman Junior next to him were determined to attack from the start to try to stop Ron Kroonder getting away from pole. By the end of the first lap they had moved up the order; Wainman was first, followed by John, Louw Wobbes, Andy Smith and Ron Kroonder. However, for the second time in three years Piet Keijzer clobbered the fence on the first turn and was hurt. The officials called for a complete restart.

This time Kroonder kept the lead at the green flag and by the end of the first lap the order was Kroonder from Wainman, Wobbes and John. John took third place on lap 5 but lost it to a hard-charging Andy Smith by halfway. John was suffering from engine trouble and dropped further back, eventually finishing in ninth, increasingly disillusioned with his Dutch experiences. He packed up to conserve his engine, choosing not to push it further in the Jac Claes Trophy or meeting final.

John had now damaged his engine three times at Baarlo, one of which, in 1990, subsequently cost him the World Final at Bradford. After a brief run of Long Track success which included victory in 1990 and second place in 1988, 1991 and 1992, John was now finding it difficult to prepare his car adequately to challenge Ron Kroonder. It was also expensive to ship the car across the English Channel each year, and unlike Peter Falding, Chris Elwell and Frankie Wainman Junior, each of whom enjoyed their Dutch travels, John was wondering whether it was worth the hassle. The following year, when British drivers were asked to declare their interest for the annual trip to Baarlo, John politely declined.

The World Final returned to Hednesford on 10th September. It was the first major championship there for three years; Hednesford was absent from the calendar in 1993 and hosted only one meeting in 1994. It was a welcome return from John's perspective; Hednesford had hosted five major championships in the five years between 1988 and 1992, and John won all five. The cover of the World Championship programme was a reminder of John's dominance. It featured a detail from a painting that commemorated the 1991 World Final, showing Bert Finnikin facing backwards and Richard Pratt flipping onto his side as John's car crossed the finish line.

John started the 1995 World Final from pole alongside Frankie Wainman Junior, the winner of the other World Semi-Final. Each had reason to be confident. Aside from his historical form at Hednesford, John went into the World Final having won both meeting finals the previous weekend and one the weekend before that. John also made up some of the distance he had lost in the technological race by borrowing a small block Chevrolet for his tarmac car, giving him the weight distribution benefits enjoyed by other small block users.

Wainman, meanwhile, seemed to be in devastating form on tarmac. Of his ten meeting final wins prior to the World Final, nine had been at tarmac tracks. Behind them, Andy Smith and Jamie Davidson made up row 2, while Paul Harrison sat on the inside of row 4 and Peter Falding lurked further back on the inside of row 8. Falding only just made it for the start and had to sprint from the pits after arriving in a helicopter from Mallory Park where he had been racing at a Eurocar meeting.

John got a good start and sneaked in front of Wainman as the green flag was waved, but overshot the first turn and ran wide, giving Wainman an easy passing opportunity. After the first couple laps, however, John realised that his car had more speed, and Wainman was pushing his car hard to stay in front. It was a similar situation to Coventry in 1993, when John was in a fast car but stuck behind Peter Falding. On that occasion John took damage as he tried to overtake and was forced to retire. So it was a brave move when John decided to repeat the same plan, attacking Wainman early in the race to seize the lead. John aimed at Wainman's back bumper and kept his car square. He hit purposely hard, wanting Wainman to go right into the fence. If he merely nudged him wide John would leave himself open to a big shunt at the end of the straight because Hednesford allowed cars to turn wide and pick up speed on the exit. Wainman was unable to avoid John's hit and smacked into a collection of stranded cars and the fence, out of the race, his World Championship ambitions over for another year. He seethed on the centre green, feeling that John had singled him out for rough treatment.

A couple of laps later Smith caught John and tried the same trick. He did not hit hard enough to knock John completely out of the race, but John did connect with the fence and lost valuable time negotiating his way out from among parked cars. By the time he rejoined he had not just been passed by Smith, but also Keith Chambers, Falding, Gaz Bott, Bob Cicconi and Murray Harrison. As the cars circled the track, John steadily gained on the five in front and felt like he would get another chance. He quickly passed Harrison, then Cicconi, who limped out of the race.

Smith's lead was also short-lived. Two laps after passing John he was slowed by traffic and an opportunity arose that Chambers seized. He hit Smith wide into two stranded cars and out of the race, the third time that a leader had been shunted from first place. That left Chambers in the lead with Falding, Bott and John trying to close the gap. John sped past Bott on a straight to take third place and focused on Falding in front. The field bunched up and the distance between cars was slashed when the marshals waved yellow flags to check that Smith was unhurt after another car collided with his stationary machine. On the restart each driver was wary of an immediate hit from behind. Perhaps because they were all concentrating on what was behind them, nobody attacked and positions remained the same after the green flag was dropped. With a bit of clear track in front of them, Chambers and Falding began to slowly draw out a lead.

John realised he was falling back and concentrated on closing the gap, driving deep into the corners and coming out like a slingshot, passing backmarkers as though they were stationary. In following such a wide racing line John must have run over a piece of debris that pierced his tyre. Two thirds of the way through the race he pulled on the centre green with a flat outside rear tyre, the same wheel that had deflated in 1993. A few laps later, Falding slowed down and pulled out with the same problem.

Chambers held on and won the race, taking the gold roof in his first major championship finish. John was left to rue his bad luck. Once he started to press the two men in front, his speed was such that he was sure would have caught Chambers and Falding before the end of the race and could have won had his tyre not let him down. It is impossible to know whether he would have been able to pass them and take the chequered flag, but it is certain that Chambers would have been forced to work harder for the win had John lasted until the end.

World Finals were usually the highlight of the season, but just occasionally they were eclipsed by a close National Points race. This was the case in 1995, when the end of the season was dominated by a three-way rivalry between John, Frankie Wainman Junior and Andy Smith that saw some tense and electrifying racing. From the start of September every race at every meeting was fiercely fought over as the three contenders sought the upper hand in the Grand Prix Series and the National Points Championship.

John started the seven-race Grand Prix Series by winning the first two meeting finals, the meetings held at Coventry and King's Lynn the weekend before the World Championship, and finishing second at the third meeting of the series at Stoke. His early lead was then chipped away by Smith, who won the third and sixth rounds. But it was Wainman who snatched the series at the last moment, winning both heats and the final in the series finale at Buxton. Smith finished second, John in third.

In a similar vein, the National Points Championship also went right down to the last meeting, with the same three drivers each with a chance of the silver roof. After his storming start to the season, Wainman lost form in August and September. That allowed John to overtake him, courtesy of victories in the meeting finals at Buxton, Coventry and King's Lynn, while Smith continued to lurk dangerously close in third place. John had one hand on the points trophy, which had eluded his grasp since 1992, but it was a weak grip.

As the season moved towards a close, Smith edged nearer to the top two with victories in the meeting final at King's Lynn on 1st October and Long Eaton on 14th October. Wainman nudged clear of him again with wins at Buxton on 15th October and Stoke on 21st October, but John retained a slim lead at the top with two second places in meeting finals. Smith then tiptoed closer with wins at Northampton on 28th October and Coventry on 4th November.

Smith went to Stoke on 5th November looking for a third consecutive meeting final win. It was a particularly frustrating occasion for John, who watched his lead in the points list dissolve.

The scrutineers barred him from racing in his heat as his car was deemed too heavy. Although he made it out for the consolation having made some quick changes, he missed on the possibility of a few extra points. Normally that would have made little difference, but with the standings so close every point counted. Wainman reminded everybody that he was still in the running for the National Points title early in the meeting final, clattering John from behind into a fence post and out of the race. John managed to fix his front and rear axles, wheels and brakes in time to get out for the Grand National, but only lasted three laps before limping to the centre green. At least he had achieved something in the race – on the second lap he returned the hit and put Wainman out of the race. John and Wainman had prevented each other scoring too many points, but the main beneficiary was Smith, who leapfrogged them both into first place in the grading list, taking a third final victory in three meetings. John almost immediately regretted bashing Wainman in the Grand National rather than racing for valuable points, but by then it was too late.

At the last meeting, at Long Eaton on 11th November, all three were still in with a chance of the National Points Championship and the silver roof. Wainman drew first blood in heat 2, which doubled up as the Grand National Championship. John was third, while Smith failed to finish. Smith still made the meeting final by winning the consolation, and in doing so became the odds-on favourite to take the National Points Championship. He just needed to finish the meeting final to build up an unassailable lead.

Wainman blitzed through the field and took an early lead, but the other superstars followed his trail. A four-car convoy developed; Wainman, Falding, Smith and John. About halfway through the race Smith pulled off a great overtaking manoeuvre, knocking both Wainman and Falding wide in one hit and taking the lead; John sneaked through for second. John needed to win the race and make sure that Smith failed to finish to send the National Points Championship down to the last race of the season, the Grand National. The next few moments would make or break both their seasons.

If ever there was need for a big hit, this was it. John needed to get close to make sure that his attack did both things it needed to; get him into first place and put Smith out of the race. As he edged closer, Wainman suddenly appeared, seemingly out of nowhere. He clattered into John, knocking him off the racing line. Although he did not put John out of the race, it allowed Smith to build up a greater lead, one that John could not catch. Wainman retired onto the centre green.

Why had Wainman taken John out? Was it payback for the World Final, where John put Wainman in the fence when he was in the lead? Whatever the reason, John was not very impressed. The grudge which first reared its head at the European and British Championships in 1992 had reignited spectacularly in 1995 and would smoulder for a few more years, creating a new stock car rivalry just as John's old opponent, Peter Falding, was becoming a less regular visitor to the racetrack.

Smith finished the meeting with 1841 points, just ahead of John's 1801 and Wainman's 1764. John had the fewest race and meeting final wins, while Wainman had the highest number of both. But in such a close finish every one of their results over the season was crucial, and both John and Wainman could point to one or two key incidents where, had luck gone their way, they would have raced under the silver roof the following year.

The race for the silver roof indicated that the balance of power had shifted. There were now three different drivers producing consistently good performances right through the season. John was still one of them, but whereas once he was the undisputed premier driver, now there were different opinions as to whether John, Wainman or Smith could claim to be the best. John's older nemesis, Peter Falding, also promised that he would be return to the track regularly in 1996.

The pressure never seemed to go away.

Paint job of a champion - an all-gold car in the Lund workshop

11

On Top of the World
1996-97

Despite missing out on the 1995 National Points Champion-ship at the last hurdle, John had little time to sulk and complain. With a wedding and honeymoon to prepare for, he had one of his busiest winters to come.

After his second marriage hit the rocks, John returned to the life of a single farmer. He met his third wife, Annette, through her father, Derek Chambers, a keen stock car racing fan. Derek raced bangers at Warton on the Lancashire-Cumbria border in the 1970s and watched Formula 1 stock cars at Nelson at the same time that John also stood on the terraces, although neither man knew the other. Derek then began to mechanic for Warren Taylor and Ray Tyldesley before joining John's team of mechanics in the early nineties.

After a period away, Annette moved home to Kendal in 1994 and started to accompany her father to stock car meetings, just as she had when she was younger. At a Coventry meeting towards the end of the season John started to chat to Annette in the bar. They got on well and there was an immediate attraction, so John asked her to a pub lunch. Since her father was part of his crew, the first date was a slightly odd double-date with Derek and his wife joining John and Annette at a local pub. Back at the farm, Annette's parents were left watching old stock car videos while John found an excuse to get Annette by herself!

A second date followed soon after, this time John arranged to pick up Annette from Kendal. Annette, who was not from a farming family, joked to her mother that John might arrive in a green Landrover – which, of course, John did! They drove off to find an articulated lorry reversing up the hill that they were descending. John decided that he could squeeze past on the pavement. He did so, but only after mangling his front wing on the side of the lorry. Despite suffering the kind of damage usually reserved for his stock car, John thought that the Landrover was fine to continue with his original plan and drove the two of them to Skipton for lunch. Nobody in the stock car world knew that they were an item, and they hoped to keep it like that for a few more weeks yet. They wandered round Skipton and bumped in to Ray Tyldesley. He made sure that their blossoming relationship was not a secret for much longer, passing it swiftly along the pits grapevine!

It was a whirlwind romance and Annette moved into the farm in a matter of weeks, soon after which John jetted off to New Zealand. Things continued well for the next few months, so John and Annette decided that John's next New Zealand trip would double up as a honeymoon. They married on 2nd January 1996 and within a few days were on a plane together bound for the other side of the world.

Their honeymoon coincided nicely with John's regular appointment at the 240 Championship. The newlyweds travelled there with a few of John's mechanics and new World Champion Keith Chambers and his crew. John had a week to get used to his new car, loaned to him by Murray West, but preparations did not go well. In his first meeting John crashed hard and was knocked out, but the officials did not realise and only stopped the race long enough to pull the car onto the centre green with John still in it. John got the car back to the pits, but he was in a bad way. He did not recognise Annette, nor knew what had happened. New Zealand rules required that a driver suffering from a concussion did not race for two weeks. That would have put John out of the 240 Championship, so his team hid him behind the transporter truck to make sure that no officials saw him. It took him all evening to come round properly, and even the next day John was unsteady.

He recovered in time for the championship weekend. The experiment of a single championship race was discarded and the meeting returned to the old familiar format, with the title decided by points accumulated over three heats. Starting on the fourth row of the grid in the first heat, John passed a couple of cars to finish in sixth place; Chambers dropped from the front row to seventeenth. Both fared worse in heat 2. Chambers retired with two punctures while John finished down the field. Things improved in the last heat; John finished in sixth place again, Chambers finished tenth. That placed John in fifth place in the overall standings, while Chambers was nineteenth.

Chambers had to acclimatise quickly to the hard style of Kiwi racing but John was a veteran of multiple trips down under. This showed in the Palmerston North Panthers v Rest of the World team race. John and Chambers were joined by two of John's former team race opponents, Lyall Rumney and Roydon Collingwood. John managed to escape a huge hit from Ross Dallas, skimming along the fence to continue racing, but Chambers was rolled by Peter McDonnell. Collingwood avoided the carnage to finish in first place and John followed him home in second to complete a comprehensive victory for the Rest of the World.

Back in the UK, John and Annette had a few short weeks to get used to married life before stock car racing took over once again. Among the early meetings was one at Wimbledon in which stock cars returned to the capital for the first time since Harringay closed in 1979. Racing in the southern half of England was dominated by Spedeworth, who promoted rival stock car models instead of BriSCA formulas. The two bodies seldom cooperated, so the Wimbledon meeting was a welcome but rare piece of collaboration between the two racing organisations.

It also gave John a chance to resume the unfinished business that he had with Frankie Wainman Junior following the conclusion of the National Points Championship the previous year. Wainman qualified for the meeting final by winning heat 1 while John scraped into the final with ninth in heat 2. Together for the first time on the grid in the final, John soon found himself in the lead with Wainman behind. Wainman waited until three-quarters distance before hitting John wide for the lead, but John recovered to get on Wainman's back bumper down the far straight. John bounced Wainman into the fence on the next corner, hard enough to put him out of the race, probably harder than was necessary. John then carried on and passed the chequered flag in first place. He felt justified in his heavy manoeuvre, seeing it as payback for wrecking his chances at the end of the previous season. The real result was that the ill-feeling between the two drivers continued to fester on.

By the time the championship events started in June, the season was beginning to take shape. John won three meeting finals in March, April and May; the one at Wimbledon was followed up with wins at Stoke and Coventry. A resurgent Peter Falding also won three meeting finals, as did Gaz Bott. Frankie Wainman Junior, Ian Platts and Matthew Bennett each won two.

John might have had even better results had he not fallen foul of the car scrutineers for the third time in three seasons. When John was found guilty of using an aluminium engine casing in 1994, it was a fair decision. When his car was deemed inside heavy at the Stoke meeting at the end of 1995, John was unsure whether the officials were correct. When his car was found to be inside heavy again in 1996, he was sure that the scrutineers were in the wrong.

Since 1994 officials had been weighing cars to check that they were balanced correctly because the advent of small block engines meant that drivers could distribute the weight across the chassis to help a car handle and turn into corners. From the start of 1996 the regulations regarding how much weight could rest on the inside and rear were made stricter.

John's shale car had a chassis that was likely to fall foul of the new regulations, so he put it aside and dragged an old car that had been slowly rusting on the farm back into his workshop. Built in 1991, raced by John for a year before being sold to the Harters who then part-exchanged it back at the end of 1992, the old car was still relatively little-used. It had been temporarily renovated by Bryce Penn, who added a coil-over suspension for the 1994 World Final, but it was then put back to pasture for eighteen months. Now John gave the car a quick once-over and decided that it needed only a thorough service and lick of paint to be in race worthy condition and competitive on track.

It certainly was. After the successes at Stoke and Coventry, the old car won the final at Bradford on 9th April. It was then that John went onto the scales in the pits and found that his car was outside the accepted tolerances. That should have been it, the scales never lie, but John pointed out several problems with the inspection. His car was weighed at the end of the race and his inside rear wheel was bent, so the bottom of the wheel had more pressure going through it. That altered the readings and made it look like the car was inside-heavy, but the scrutineers would not let John change the wheel and re-weigh the car. John was also confident that the scales were faulty, a fact that would be proved by Frankie Wainman Junior at a later race meeting. When Wainman was told that his car was considerably out of tolerance, he argued that the scales were on a slope and the low side would read heavy. When he took his car off the scales and reversed back on, the readings were completely different and this time the other side of the car seemed to be too heavy.

John took the disqualification with more grace than it warranted, but inwardly he was fuming. He was prepared to swear by his car's legality and was convinced that the problem was with the equipment, but there was so much finger-pointing from the officials that John thought he would have no chance of persuading the authorities. Later, with hindsight, he would wish that he had been more vocal in his defence. Were he a naturally vociferous personality – a Stuart Smith, perhaps – he would have done, and probably got the judgement overturned. But John was a milder, gentler sort. Instead he took the punishment and made sure that he weighed his car on the official scales at the start of each meeting to double check that his car complied with the regulations before the scrutineers could call him to account.

John needed to ensure that the weight distribution was unquestionably legal since he was using only one car. Early in the season he sold his tarmac car, the one that had caused problems with the aluminium engine casing over the past three seasons, to Chris Lloyd. It left John using his shale car, already an old model, on both surfaces for the remainder of the season. His tarmac engine, which was not part of the sale to Lloyd, was switched to what was now John's only race worthy car.

John's relationship with the officials improved at Stoke on 20th April, when he won the meeting final and was promoted to first in the Grand National after Gaz Bott was deemed to have cut across the infield illegally. Two weeks later, at Coventry, John took out Jamie Davidson and Andy Smith on the last lap to take victory there. Two final wins boosted him up the grading list.

John returned to Coventry for the British Championships on 1st June and finished his two heats in seventh and fourth. Since Peter Falding had a first and fifth, Andy Smith had a first and third and Frankie Wainman Junior had two seconds, John thought that he was too far back on the grid to have any real hope in the championship race. Despite his fears he made it to third place with three laps to go, behind Falding and Paul Harrison, but a flat tyre destroyed any hopes of a win or even a podium finish and forced John to watch the last couple of laps from the centre green. His next chance for success came at the European Championship, but he had a disappointing weekend. He did not finish the championship race in the top ten, and his best result in nine races over the weekend meeting was fifth place.

After such a poor return at the British and European Championships, and with no Long Track Championship to distract him, it looked like John might be about to finish another season without a major trophy. But his attention was now firmly on the World Championship. He went to the World Semi-Final at King's Lynn, started from pole position and led to the chequered flag. A very greasy track meant that most of his opponents drove cautiously, and John was little troubled en route to the win.

The result gave John a front row spot for the World Final at Coventry. He lined up on the outside, with Ian Platts to his left. The most dangerous opponents nearby were Paul Harrison, on the inside of row 2, and Frankie Wainman Junior, on the inside of row 4. Peter Falding failed to qualify, Andy Smith scraped in through the Consolation Semi-Final and was adrift on the back row, defending champion Keith Chambers languished back on row 14.

The Coventry shale was, as usual, a difficult surface to race on. It was slippery, like driving on eggshells, and it was easy to lose traction in a corner. John's outside line as the green flag fell meant that he was in loose shale and a fountain of dirt erupted from his outside rear tyre as his Hoosier fought for grip. On the inside rows it was even worse. The watered track had little loose shale on it and Platts struggled even more for traction. John nosed in front down the home straight and kept the lead through the first turn.

By halfway through the race, Platts had dropped out and John's major challenger was Harrison. He kept up with John as the leader sliced through traffic and saw his chance arise when John was momentarily delayed by Berry Paardekooper. Harrison launched himself at John's car and hit it, but Paardekooper sponged the momentum of the impact and John maintained the racing line. John sped down the back straight with Harrison now falling back. The impact had caused minor damage to Harrison's radiator and his engine was no longer running at full power.

John managed to keep control of his car for the last five laps and brought it home first, ahead of Harrison and Wainman. It was his fifth World Final victory. Despite the ructions over weight distribution, running a single car and his poor performances at the British and European Championships, John proved that he could still be the best driver on the biggest occasions.

Previously, John's World Final winnings were ploughed back into the car to make it even better. This time, it was different. John and Annette both wanted children and the prize money went towards IVF treatment. The supportive husband drove Annette to

Newcastle for her first appointment, and ever the romantic, took her on a tour of industrial estate to point out the location of the old Aycliffe stock car track. Annette chose to go to her other appointments alone after that!

Back under the gold roof for a fifth time, John did not replicate his World Final success at the rest of the regular season meetings. The closest he came was second place in two meeting finals, at King's Lynn and Coventry. John was off the pace in the Grand Prix Series, not attending two of the ten meetings and failing to finish in another round.

The end of the season was not as exciting as the climactic finish of 1995. John's lack of victories meant that Frankie Wainman Junior took the National Points Championship with 1719 points, ahead of John on 1482 and Peter Falding on 1372. John's four meeting finals were eclipsed by Wainman's eight and Falding's seven; defending champion Andy Smith managed seven meeting finals to get fifth place in the championship. John was above him by virtue of his superior meeting attendance and consistent race finishes. But he still had the thing that all the others wanted most of all: the gold roof.

As usual the off-season was interrupted by a trip to New Zealand and the 240 Championship. John and his team were joined by the biggest contingent yet making the long journey to the other side of the world; the British challenge included Frankie Wainman Junior, Russell Taylor, Gaz Bott, Clinton Dorrell and Shane Dorrell. John was driving a car owned by Murray West, a good machine which had made it to fifth place in the New Zealand Championships only a week before.

The 240 Championship not only required a good car, it needed excellent driving and a good slice of luck to avoid the inevitable on-track carnage. John finished twelfth in the first heat and fifth in the second, which gave him fifth place in the overall standings going into the last race. Wainman led the standings after finishing second and third in the first two heats. Both were bound to be the focus of attention going into the decider. It was John who fell first, drilled into the wall by Barry Hunter. John's car was towed onto the centre green, his chance of the title gone. Now all eyes turned to the other foreigner with a chance of taking the title from New Zealand. Wainman survived largely unscathed until the last corner, where he was taken onto the infield by Ian King, but he kept his engine running and crossed the line in fourth. That was enough to keep him at the top of the pile, the second British winner of the 240 Championship after Chris Elwell's victory at the maiden event in 1987. John was the second-placed Brit in fourteenth, Gaz Bott was twentieth, Shane Dorrell twenty-first; Russell Taylor and Clinton Dorrell did not score.

The 240 Championship had eluded him again, but John began the British 1997 season knowing that he was just one win away from Stuart Smith's record of six World Final victories. John always aimed at the World Final, but now it was surely even more of a target. Yet the defending World Champion and most successful current driver shocked many by suggesting that he might be prepared to turn his back on BriSCA stock car racing in favour of an alternative formula.

Gaz Bott, an experienced red top driver who was in the middle of the two best seasons of his career, was unhappy with the political management of the sport and had seen a few things in New Zealand that had got his mind churning. Soon after he returned, he began to test the waters for a new formula of stock cars he called Supermodifieds. John went along to a test meeting at Hednesford. Bott had persuaded a clutch of top drivers to attend his test rather than go to the regular Long Eaton fixture, proving that he had captured the attention of those at the top of the sport.

John's interest in the Supermodified formula stemmed from the fact that much of Bott's problem with BriSCA racing was related to tyres. Hoosier gave Bott a selection of big, wide racing tyres, a type banned under Formula 1 regulations. Bott wanted to test the new tyres on a range of current stock cars. John thought that his own car was not much quicker at the test meeting, nor did he see much improvement among his opponents. He did, however, think that drivers would be able to alter their setup if they had access to the tyres over a longer period, and the Hoosiers would then lead to quicker lap times.

The Supermodifieds were never likely to be anything more than a passing phase. John's interest was little more than curiosity and there was never any real threat that he would move away from BriSCA. He was committed to his current formula and wanted to achieve all that he could in the sport with which he had been involved for more than two decades.

Nothing has ever tempted John away from stock cars. He had a crack in Jimmy Wallace's Formula 2 at the end of 1988, but that was only a one-off where the Formula 1 and 2 World Champions borrowed each other's cars for a meeting. Neither enjoyed much success since they did not have the experience in car setup that they had in their usual formula. John also gave Wallace a bit of a headache by planting the Formula 2 in the Aycliffe fence, sending the car back in worse condition than he received it! Being World Champion also gave John the opportunity to try other forms of motorsport too. He was persuaded to try Formula Ford cars at Donington and enjoyed the experience, but remained convinced that stock car racing was superior. Whereas Formula Ford drivers were constrained by extremely strict regulations and rules, stock car drivers could alter their car to seek an advantage. John was also shocked by the cost and expense involved in running a Formula Ford. Stock cars remained one of the few motorsports where a driver could build a car in his own workshop and still be competitive. In addition, John was frustrated in the Formula Ford when he got stuck behind another car, regretting that he could not use his front bumper to move the other car out of the way!

While John was experimenting with Gaz Bott's new developments, he continued with his old car on both surfaces. John had initially intended to renovate a spare, unused car for tarmac. It was gradually refurbished during spare moments in 1996 and loaned to Rowan Yandle for the World Final at Coventry. The car ran well and looked like it would be a good addition to John's armoury, but others had noticed it too. John received a good offer from Holland after the World Final and sold it. Since the World Championship was to be held on shale for the second year in a row, John decided to race in 1997 with a single car again. After all, it had proved successful in 1996, winning the World Final. All that changed for the new season was a replacement front axle.

John started the 1997 season in positive fashion. He won a meeting final in each of the first three months of the season; at Bradford in March, Long Eaton in April and Bradford in May. Those results were complemented by four second places in meeting finals. That good form took John to the British Championship, held at Buxton on 21st June, in a confident mood. Being isolated in the Peak District and away from decent road links, Buxton was struggling to attract drivers. This meeting was no different; only 27 drivers attended and each drove in two out of three heats. John won the first heat and finished sixth in his second, but was knocked off the front row of the championship grid by Frankie Wainman Junior and Keith Chambers, who each won a heat and finished fifth in their other. Jamie Davidson and Andy Smith also qualified well, leaving John on the inside of row 3.

The heats were punctuated by rain. Conditions cleared for the championship race, although it remained gloomy and overcast.

John selected a Hoosier Dirt Stocker, typically a shale tyre, for the inside rear wheel. Although it was a maverick choice, it paid off on a slippery track. The slick surface caught out Chambers, who spun onto the infield, and Smith, who was sent into the fence by Wainman. That left Wainman out in front, followed by Davidson and John. Wainman and Davidson sparred for the lead; Davidson got in front on lap 5 and Wainman retook him on lap 7. When Davidson attacked again on lap 8 he got it wrong, sending both cars wide, allowing John to take the inside line into the lead. John stayed secure in first place until the end of the race; Gaz Bott and Ray Witts joined him on the podium. It was the fifth time that John was British Champion. What made it more special was that all the other front-runners used tarmac specials but John was more than competitive in his multi-surface car, although the wet conditions did much to level the playing field.

The World Semi-Finals sandwiched the European Championship in a busy three weekends in July. John was given pole position in the first World Semi-Final at Long Eaton. The qualification rankings did John a favour since Frankie Wainman Junior, Andy Smith, Paul Harrison, Peter Falding and Keith Chambers all lined up in the second World Semi-Final. As most predicted, John ran home in first place in the weaker field, ahead of fellow front rower Jamie Davidson.

With the pressure of World Final qualification lifted, John went to the European Championship at Northampton in a relaxed frame of mind. This time he was not able to repeat the tarmac heroics he had displayed to take the British title. John needed a wet track to keep up with the front runners in their tarmac-specific cars, but the clouds failed to open. Keith Chambers won the title for the second season in a row, finishing ahead of Frankie Wainman Junior and Gaz Bott. John was just off the podium in fourth.

Those busy July weekends were followed by an uncommon-ly-quiet August, when John raced in only two out of ten race meetings. He chose to save his car for shale and sat out the tar-mac meetings at Northampton, Skegness (twice), Buxton and Birmingham. At Coventry on 2nd August, dubbed the Heart of England Championship, John finished his two heats in fifth and second and the final in ninth. His other August meeting, at Stoke on 23rd August, was more successful. A lack of cars meant that John raced in two heats again, finishing second in both, then first in the final. At least the shortage of cars was not as chronic as at Buxton the following day. Only six drivers were in attendance and Jamie Davidson picked up what must have been the easiest victory of his career.

John spent plenty of time in the workshop leading up to the World Final after Ray Tyldesley collided with him at Coventry on 7th September, leaving him with a severely damaged rear axle, suspension and gearbox. Since John only had one car at his disposal, he needed to get it fixed fast. A test run at Long Eaton a week later saw John finish only the consolation in seventh. He now had two weeks to fine tune his setup, which had been worked to perfection on shale before the Coventry incident. Now John would go to the World Championships with a suspect car.

The packed grid in the other World Semi-Final meant that the front of the World Final grid lacked one or two big names. Keith Chambers failed to qualify, Paul Harrison had to accept one of the Consolation Semi-Final slots. Peter Falding nearly didn't make it too, but third place in the Consolation Semi-Final made him the first reserve and he was allowed onto the back row when Gaz Bott was forced to pull out before the race. That left Andy Smith on the front row alongside John. Between them they had won the previous two Bradford-hosted World Finals. Frankie Wainman Junior was behind John on the inside of row 2.

John had to put all doubts about his car at the back of his mind for the race. He matched Smith down the home straight as the green flag fell and held the inside line through the first corner to keep the lead. Smith was forced to defend second position from Wainman and soon retired after Wainman forced him into a backmarker.

That allowed Wainman to concentrate on catching John, who was carefully picking his way through the traffic. Wainman was soon close to John's rear, and on lap 13 he nudged John wide and went into the lead. It was unfortunate for Wainman that waved yellow flags brought the race to a temporary halt within seconds, allowing John to recover and attack on the restart, but Wainman got away well when the green flags waved again and pulled away to create a half-lap advantage. John then gradually reeled him back in. He was closing the gap using his tried and trusted Bradford technique, pushing hard into the corner and going right up to the fence so he could pick up speed on the straights. After a few laps of chasing hard he was close to Wainman, near enough to attack if he wanted to. John waited for the right moment, but six laps from the end John went too wide and his wheel sank into a bank of soft shale high on the corner. He lost traction and direction, slipping down the track until he found enough grip to correct his line round the corner. It meant that John lost all the ground that he had made up over the previous laps, and he had to begin again – but this time with the end of the race almost in sight.

Wainman was now the strong favourite, but the constant pressure from John earlier in the race meant that he had to push his car hard. Now his tyres were beginning to deteriorate, whereas John's setup was kinder to tyres and his remained in optimum condition. The gap closed a second time, but much quicker than before. To add to Wainman's problems, he was delayed by a Dutch driver who sheared across the track onto the infield, running in front of the leader. The small collision did no damage to Wainman's car but it cost him valuable time. John was now right on Wainman's back bumper and hit him going into the next turn. His wheel locked onto Wainman's side and for a fraction of a second it looked like both cars would be out of the race, but they separated and John dived into the lead. With his tyres in better condition, John opened up enough of a gap to be safe from a desperate last-lap lunge. John passed the chequered flag in first place to win the World Final.

Wainman had to settle for second place, his attempt to get the gold roof beaten by John again. Falding, in an amazing drive, leapt to third place despite starting from the back of the grid. But the story of the World Final was all about John's victory. As he jumped out of the car at the end of the race, John realised that he had achieved something special. Stuart Smith was one of the first to shake John's hand, a sign of congratulation from one six-time World Champion to another. John had equalled Smith's tally of World Final wins.

John's absences from the grid in August meant that he had little chance of success in the National Points Championship and Frankie Wainman Junior romped to victory. He had a near thousand point lead over second-placed John, 2263 to 1314. Andy Smith was third with 1057 points. Peter Falding had cut back on racing again, and drifted back to ninth in the grading list.

Although he had won 21 races, the same number as the previous year, John had doubled his number of meeting final victories, winning eight. He won one meeting in each calendar month of the season except one: March at Bradford, April at Long Eaton, May at Bradford, June at Buxton (the British Championship), July at Coventry, August at Stoke, October at Bradford and November at Stoke. In the month that he did not win a meeting final, September, John won the World Championship.

John was struggling to compete with Frankie Wainman Junior in many of the regular race meetings that made up the National Points Championship, but the race for the silver roof never bothered him. What motivated John was the fight for every single race and meeting final – and if he lost, he moved onto the next one. And if that next meeting was a major championship, that was even better. That way, John might continue to add to his outstanding tally of titles.

Leading the revolution - a radical new look for 1999

12

Innovator
1998-1999

As a six-time World Champion, John could easily justify turning out on track in a car bearing number 1. Stuart Smith was given the honour of wearing number 1 from 1981 (at which point he had won three World Finals) until his retirement, and Peter Falding raced under number 1 for the year that he held the gold roof after the 1993 World Final. John was also offered the chance to switch to number 1 while he was the reigning World Champion, but it says something about his modesty that he elected to stay faithful to 53. That was the number that had served him well since 1976, and it is the number that will remain forever associated with him.

John's modesty carried over into the pits. New drivers were astounded when they first met him. They had followed John's career, watching him battle with Ray Leigh, Ian Higgins, Peter Falding and Frankie Wainman Junior. Aggressive use of the bumper and the trademark Lund lunge on the last bend gave them the impression that John would be loud, confident, even cocky. But he was very different off the track to how he was on it. John was a quiet, modest, thoughtful type. Often, when asked a question, he would pause before answering as though he was going over the response in his head. John would help out fellow drivers when they asked him for advice, few went away from his transporter bus dissatisfied.

John had always been the same, right from the first time he raced, but fatherhood matured him even more. James and Sam were now eleven and nine, and they had two half-siblings on the way. Following the success of the World Final funded IVF treatment, Annette gave birth to twin daughters, Abbie and Amy, on 1st March 1998. Their arrival spurred John into selling his sheep, choosing to concentrate solely on cattle, so that the lambing season could pass without John spending long nights on the sofa.

Annette's pregnancy meant that John missed the 240 Championship in New Zealand that year, so he was eager to get back on track by the time the British season started on 4th April. He tasted victory at Coventry in the first race meeting of the season, taking first place in the meeting final as well as second place in the consolation and Grand National. Frankie Wainman Junior then snatched back first place in the grading list with three meeting final victories in April and May, while John had to settle for four podium places.

Things went even better at the British Championship at Coventry on 6th June. John won a place on the outside of the front row of the grid courtesy of a win and a second place in his two heats. Frankie Wainman Junior started from pole after two wins; Richard Mason and Andy Smith started on row 2. When the green flag fell in the championship race, John stomped hard on the accelerator. His car skewed to the left and looked like it might spin, but his tyres gripped and he shot off towards the inside line of the first turn. Space opened up there as Wainman missed a gear change and momentarily held up the pack behind him. It gave John breathing space for the first few laps, after which Wainman began to close in.

Wainman was suffering from a damaged suspension but still looked to have an advantage in terms of straight-line speed. He was very close when John came across Phil Smith spinning on the home straight with only a few laps to go. John put his foot down again and struck Smith's rear bumper, spinning him out of the way. Wainman closed in further, but his collapsed suspension meant that he settled for second rather than risk causing more damage. John came home in first, now a six-time British Champion to match his six World Championships and National Points Championships.

John started from pole position in the first of the World Semi-Finals which was held at Skegness on 27th June. Unlike the previous year, John faced a stronger competition for the best spots on the World Final grid. Paul Harrison completed the front row, Keith Chambers and Andy Smith sat just behind on row 2. In a cautious, careful race, fifteen of twenty starters finished. John led from start to finish, almost untouched by any other car, followed by Smith, John Cayzer, Harrison and Chambers. John then went on to take the chequered flag first in the meeting final, and did the same seven days later at Coventry.

If the World Semi-Final was a merry-go-round in which the front runners were happy to take few risks, the European Championship on 19th July was anything but. Only six cars finished the championship race and John was not one of them; he rode the kerb and picked up a flat tyre in trying to avoid a pile-up at the end of the far straight. Paul Harrison was one of the few to avoid trouble and took the title. It was not a complete failure since John came second in the meeting final, driving over the line with a flat tyre having collided with the fence in a last chance effort to try and wallop Peter Falding out of the way to win. He also won the World of Shale race and meeting final at Stoke the following weekend.

The World Championship was held at Coventry on 19th September. John was happy with the choice of venue. He had won the World Final the last time it came to Coventry, in 1996, and he had won three out of six meetings so far in 1998, including the British Championship. Moreover, he was starting from pole position. Frankie Wainman Junior started alongside, looking for his first World Final win.

John got off to a good start and was soon in the lead and among the backmarkers. It all seemed to be going well until he passed Stan Hickey, a New Zealand entrant, on the home straight. Despite being a lap down, Hickey clattered into the back of John on the next corner and smacked him into a stationary car. John took damage to his tyre and retired when it deflated.

The fact that Hickey was driving a car loaned from Frankie Wainman Junior was not lost on many spectators, who complained that Hickey's attack was unfair, born of Kiwi-style team racing so that Wainman might win. That might be an over-exaggeration, but it was certainly an example of the different ways that drivers race on opposite sides of the world. In the UK, backmarkers rarely trouble cars that are a lap ahead of them. In New Zealand, nobody is safe and backmarkers regularly attack drivers who are a lap in front.

Whatever the reasons behind it, Hickey's manoeuvre stopped John rewriting the record books. His chance for three consecutive World Championships had gone again. Frankie Wainman Junior took the chequered flag instead, finally winning the World Final after seven years at the top of the sport.

John finished the season with two second places in meeting finals and a win in the Grand National Championship at the last meeting of the season at Coventry. It was another success in John's most productive competition. Never mind his six World, British and National Points titles; it was John's eighth victory in the Grand National Championship.

Frankie Wainman Junior was a deserved winner of the National Points Championship again with 1687 points. John finished second for the fourth consecutive season with 1099 points, while Andy Smith was third with 782. Wainman had won eleven meeting finals to John's five and had far more race wins, 48 to 14.

Wainman dominated in meetings where there were fewer drivers in attendance, giving his faster car more space to manoeuvre. Between April and July he won eight finals, at which the highest number of drivers at a meeting was 29. John won his five finals in the same period, but at the meetings where he was successful there were 68, 63, 61, 65 and 40 drivers. John had lost some of his speed and tended to win races when the track was more crowded, making use of his skill and experience to work his way through the field.

John went back to New Zealand in 1999 hoping for success in the 240 Championship, but he had use of an uncompetitive Scott Myers car that was never close to matching the pace of the leaders. Nevertheless, it was fast and sturdy enough to help John achieve one thing: revenge. After finishing fourteenth in heat 1 and fifteenth in heat 2, John raced in heat 3 and found himself behind Stan Hickey, the driver who had wrecked his World Final. The temptation was too much to bear. John launched himself at Hickey, sending the New Zealander halfway over the pit wall.

John motored on past, well down in the final standings, but satisfied with a job well done!

Annette did not join him in New Zealand on that occasion since the twins were too young for such a long journey. She waited at home for her husband's return. It was cold and snowy in Lancashire when John rang to report that his plane had been delayed due to a cracked windscreen, and he would be stranded for a couple of days in Sydney. While Annette cursed the weather back home, John had the bonus of two days at Bondi Beach!

Perhaps the unexpected break gave John time to think over his plans for the new season. Realising that Wainman had leapfrogged him in the technological race and was running quicker cars, John decided to try something new over the winter. He sold his 1996 and 1997 World Final winning car and its big block engine to Stuart Trousdale. To replace it, ten years after his opponents first tried it, John built a car that housed a small block engine. Yet John did not want to merely catch up to the pack, he wanted to gain a competitive edge over his rivals. He looked for a new innovation to make the best use of the small block engine and to make the Lund car the fastest on track again.

One option was based on what he had seen in New Zealand, where cars were built using a space frame chassis. Space frame construction used blocks of steel with thinner walls and allowed New Zealand drivers to offset their engines and run with lower bumpers. John considered the various benefits of the space frame chassis, but decided that it would not suit the British tracks. The first and most important reason was that the space frame layout would involve more cost and complication. John did not have the time to deal with the many construction issues that would inevitably arise with a new building technique, nor the repairs that would be necessary when the car was damaged. Second, the

British roll cage regulations required a specific type of steel tubing which would be difficult to weld to a space frame chassis. Third, the main benefit gained from a space frame chassis – the ability to offset the engine – was hampered by British regulations on weight distribution. John dropped the idea of space frame building and it was left to Frankie Wainman Junior to pioneer a British space frame chassis car the following year.

John had another trick up his sleeve, again inspired by New Zealand cars. He decided to build a chassis with a short wheelbase, ten inches shorter than the traditional 100 inches. Short and squat, with downtubes connecting the top of the roll cage, bonnet and bumper, the car looked like nothing else on the grid. Even the familiar Lund cab design, unchanged since 1978, was gone. Another new innovation involved the brake callipers, which were mounted on the rear axle bird cages rather than on the axle itself to make the car more stable when braking. As if to symbolise the change to a new style of car, John painted the body silver. Since 1979 he had raced in a white car, now he was returning to the colour used in the first three years of his career. He put all his eggs in one basket and used the same car on both shale and tarmac. That was a brave decision considering he was venturing into the unknown with such a radical new design.

John hoped that his short car would handle better, but the experimentation process to get the new car set up correctly was slow and often exasperating. At times the car was very quick, but on other occasions it was awful. The rear suspension was problematic in the first few weeks, followed by weight issues, rear brake problems and dodgy shock absorbers. Not even the return of Belle Vue to the schedule helped John to succeed, and his best result there was fourth place in the inaugural meeting final. It was a different stadium and track to the one that John enjoyed in the seventies and eighties, but the resurrection of Belle Vue was welcomed by the drivers and fans who remembered the old atmospheric track.

Not until the penultimate meeting of the season did John win a meeting final. It nearly came much earlier, on 31st May at Sheffield, but John came second. He led on the far straight on the last lap, but Frankie Wainman Junior cleverly nipped round the inside as John drifted wide on the last bend, expecting a hit. Instead John had to wait until 31st October, at Sheffield again. Yet Sheffield was a tight shale track that did not rely on high speed, so John's win there was not a signal that he had the car finally sorted.

The championship events were frustrating. John was close to success, only to falter at the key moment. He first threatened the podium at the UK Open Championship. John led the final on the last lap and looked to have a big enough gap to escape a last-bend lunge from second placed Paul Harrison. The challenger still went for it and made contact halfway round the turn, sending both cars into the fence. Harrison got moving first and crossed the line to win, while John was unable to get going again and watched the rest of the field file past him.

John won a heat at the British Championship despite trailing home behind Andy Smith. The scrutineers were doing their rounds of the pits again and Smith's car was outside the weight distribution tolerances. He was deleted from the results, despite claims from Smith that the scales were incorrect. John finished third in another heat, giving him third place on the grid behind yellow top Clinton Dorrell and the old hand Frankie Wainman Senior. However, John failed to finish the championship race. He was whacked by Dorrell on lap 2, taking both out of the race together with Wainman, and it was Frankie Wainman Junior who worked his way through for the win. The fact that Dorrell was related to the Wainmans by marriage opened up accusations that the Wainman clan was indulging in team racing, doing what they could to take out John and give Frankie Wainman Junior the best chance to win. Coupled with Stan Hickey taking John out of the 1998 World Final, the charge against the Wainmans was beginning to look more convincing.

Any suggestion that there was a murky conspiracy emanating from the Wainman transporter was wide of the mark. John and Wainman were on better terms than the days when the rivalry between them was at its height in 1995. What was clear, however, was that Clinton Dorrell seemed to have a personal grudge against John and singled him out for rough treatment on track. He had taken John out of the meeting final at Coventry when a lap down the year before, and his brother Shane had rammed John when he was stuck in the fence at Swaffham. As the most successful driver out on track, John was bound to be a target of a maverick who wanted to impose themselves on a race. Whereas in past years he might have retaliated and tried to strike back, even at the detriment of race position, John allowed Clinton Dorrell to get on with whatever he had in mind and concentrated on his own race. The furore died down after Dorrell was universally castigated for ruining what might have been a great race, and John could concentrate on winning – something at which Dorrell was not close to matching him.

At the European Championship, John did not trouble the field. He retired early again, leaving Murray Harrison to win from Andy Smith and Peter Falding. That left only the World Championship. John's struggles with his new car meant that he did not fare so well in the qualifying meetings. For the first time in years he did not have one of the two best qualifying scores and did not start his World Semi-Final from pole position. At least he was still on the front row, alongside Frankie Wainman Junior. Few expected John to retain a top two slot on the Northampton tarmac since his new car seemed to struggle there more than anywhere else, but the two front rowers remained in the top spots at the chequered flag, Wainman first and John second. Peter Falding finished third and would take up a dangerous spot on row 4 in the World Final. It was another typical World Semi-Final with few incidents as the top drivers made sure that they finished safely. As far as John was concerned, he had got over a major hurdle and was pleased with his car's performance.

Coventry was host to the World Final for the second year in a row. Although John's form had dropped off earlier in the season, he felt like he was turning the corner and was getting his new car running more reliably and consistently. For the first time in months, he felt like a genuine contender. Andy Smith started from pole with Frankie Wainman Junior alongside him. John lined up on the inside of the second row, with the season's surprise package, Murray Harrison, on the outside.

The start was all about the two men on the front row. Smith and Wainman battled for the best line into the first corner; Smith came out on top. John and Harrison went by too, dropping Wainman back to fourth. Smith then went wide on the first turn of lap 2, tamely allowing John to take the lead. At quarter-distance, Murray Harrison lost control as he rounded the backmarkers, allowing Wainman and Paul Harrison through for third and fourth; Murray recovered for fifth. Three laps later, John came a cropper at the same part of the track. Ian Higgins dived from the outside to inside to avoid an out of control Ray Williams and sideswiped John, who spun onto the centre green. John rejoined in fifth; Smith, Wainman and both Harrisons got past.

Halfway through the race, in drying conditions, Wainman's car seemed to pick up speed. At the same time, John worked his way past Murray Harrison while Paul Harrison retired with broken steering. Smith and Wainman now enjoyed a healthy lead ahead of John, who opened up his own gap in front of Murray Harrison.

With five laps to the finish, Smith lost traction and Wainman took the inside line into the lead. Smith would not let him go quietly and repeatedly attacked, but each time Wainman did just enough to ride the hit and stay in the lead. Their scuffle allowed John to get back in touch, although John was concerned that Smith was struggling to stay on Wainman's rear. John decided to make his move, otherwise Wainman would get away to win and Smith would concentrate on blocking John in third place. John decided to try and pass them both at once.

The starter signalled two laps to go. John kept his foot on the accelerator as the three cars motored down the straight. He wanted to hit Smith hard enough that he would domino into Wainman, knocking both cars wide. However, Smith did not slow for the corner as John expected. He had decided to attack Wainman on the very same corner and kept his speed up, aiming at Wainman's back bumper. Smith contacted with Wainman and knocked him wide and sideways. John was relying on Smith to slow him down, now there was nothing there to stop him. John followed Smith wide and eventually hit him late, high on the corner. Smith cannoned back into Wainman and John followed. The collision knocked John into the air and he climbed above them both, teetering on top of Smith's bonnet. Luckily his engine kept running. Still in gear, John found traction on something and bounced off the crashed cars. Then, as he hit the track, his engine stalled.

After what seemed like an age, Harrison came pottering past, taking the inside line through the corner slowly and cautiously. John got his engine running again, but had a flat tyre which slowed him considerably. That allowed Frankie Wainman Senior, who was enjoying something of a late-career resurgence, to get past John and leave him in third place. It stayed that way until the end. Smith managed to ease himself away from the crash but only for eleventh place.

John had a podium position, but left feeling hard done by. The choice to attack both Smith and Frankie Wainman Junior was not the wrong one. He was not to know that Smith had chosen the same corner for his attempt. If John had held back and let Smith hit Wainman, he would probably have sneaked through the inside and into the lead, but hindsight is a wonderful thing. John was third with Murray Harrison the surprise winner. The popular driver had won both European and World Championships in a season in which he won no other meeting finals and only eight races overall.

There was no disguising that it had been a hard year for John, although he had got his radical new car running better by the end of the season. As well as his solitary meeting final win at Sheffield, he took three other podium places in his final seven meetings and second place in the Grand National Championship. Rob Perry took the Grand National crown; John's last bend attack was not enough to take the lead and retain the title. Yet despite his late successes, John unsurprisingly slipped back in the National Points Championship. Frankie Wainman Junior was a clear winner again, this time ahead of Andy Smith. John dropped from third place to fourth in the final grading period, losing his place to Ray Witts by just three points. It was the first time he was outside the top three in the season-long battle for points since 1985.

And that may have been it, the end of the story; the end of a career. John had just one car, and received a good offer for it from another driver who thought that he could turn the short wheelbase into a winner. John considered accepting the cash and walking away from the sport. Nobody would blame him. He was now 45, had a young family and a busy farm to run. He had achieved almost everything that could be achieved in the sport that he had dominated for the past fifteen years. He could give it all up and watch the races as a casual spectator, chewing the cud with Stuart Smith and Willie Harrison in the bar. Perhaps it was time to leave it to a younger generation.

The undisputed champion after the 2002 World Final

13

Record Breaker
2000-2002

To sell or not to sell? That was the question.

John asked the advice of those closest to him, but the decision had to be his alone. Ever thoughtful, John weighed up the pros and cons of retiring. Ultimately one thing swayed his decision. John was a family man first, a stock car driver second. Yet stock cars provided an environment in which his family thrived. What else, he thought, could bring the family together more than travelling as a group to race meetings? At most race meetings the transporter bus included John, Annette, the twins, John's sons, Annette's father and Pete Billows, John's cousin and long term mechanic. His stock car was the magnet that brought them together.

The decision was made. The offer was refused.

John still had to come to terms with slipping back in the National Points Championship. Maybe the new millennium was an appropriate time for a new approach to racing. John decided that 2000 would see him back on track in two cars, one for each surface. He began to prepare a new shale car, returning closer to the traditional 100 inch wheelbase and chassis design with a car that measured 96 inches. The extra space was needed to fit the big block engine originally used in the mid-nineties tarmac car that was sold to Chris Lloyd. John wanted to return to the old reliable power blocks that had driven him to success in the past. The advantage of a small block engine was far reduced on shale, where cornering required less braking and acceleration. Not all the new ideas from the short wheelbase car were discarded, most notably the rear brake callipers mounted on bird cages.

The annual New Zealand trip delayed the completion of the new machine, but it was something that John did not want to turn down because he might pick up some hints on how to improve his short wheelbase car. He returned over the winter for another shot at the 240 Championship, joined by Frankie Wainman Junior, Murray Harrison and Jason Holden. John raced from the back of the grid in heat 1 and progressed through the field, but tangled with Rodney Wood and dropped back down to finish sixteenth. His worst grid position out of the way, John could now concentrate on better results in the next two heats. In the second heat he finished fourth, followed by second position in heat 3. That was good enough for fourth place in the overall standings, although a mistake from the scorers meant that he was originally presented with the third place trophy. It was an excellent year for the Brits overall: Wainman's finishes of second, third and fifth won him the title for the second time, Harrison was fifth and Holden fourteenth.

The intention was that the radical short wheelbase car used the previous year would be converted to tarmac-only racing, although the New Zealand trip ate into the winter break and the new shale car was further delayed as John struggled to find suitable axles. The tarmac car temporarily remained in use on both surfaces until John charged the Sheffield fence on 24th April in it. The impact jarred the engine and finding the source of a vibration caused some headaches in the workshop.

The new shale car was then rushed to completion and made its debut on 13th May. Now the new machine had to double up on tarmac temporarily until the fault with the tarmac car was diagnosed and dealt with. The new car's first outing was on tarmac at Skegness, but John failed to overcome the inevitable teething problems and did not finish. The following day, John was back on the Skegness track for the UK Open Championship. This time he qualified for the meeting final with third in his heat, but failed to finish the final.

Despite the disjointed start to the season, two second places and a third place in the meeting finals of the World Championship qualifying meetings gave John a spot on the inside of the second row of the World Semi-Final grid at Swaffham. One of the men in front of him was to be expected; Frankie Wainman Junior had won multiple heats in the qualifying rounds. The other was a new driver who carried a fearsome reputation. Rob Speak transferred to Formula 1 stock cars after dominating Formula 2 for a decade in the nineties. His roll of honour eclipsed even John. Eleven-time consecutive National Points Champion, eight-time World Champion, quadruple British Champion and double European Champion; Speak had done it all in the junior, lower-budget formula. He was now ready to try his hand in the big league. After a few test races in 1998 and 1999, he announced his arrival in 2000 with victory in four meeting finals in the eleven World Championship qualifying events.

With two excellent drivers in front of him, John knew that it was asking a lot to win and take a front row spot in the World Final. Wainman took off from the start to keep the lead, Speak settled in behind for second and John easily kept third since fellow second-rower Murray Harrison was racing his shale car on tarmac after a midweek engine implosion in his other machine. As the top three steadily circled the track, none seemed willing to risk any heroics. John realised that he had more pace than Speak and nudged him aside for second, but was not prepared to leave himself open to retribution by attacking the faster Wainman. At the end of the race, John was happy to place in second. Wainman won, happy with the debut of his new space frame chassis tarmac car. Speak had to settle for third.

Prior to the World Semi-Final, John kept his season ticking over with four race meetings in each of June and July. Among them was the British Championship, where John qualified for the championship race with second place in a heat, but he failed to finish his other so started down the grid. He was in good company: Rob Speak, Paul Harrison, Frankie Wainman Junior and John made up rows 7 and 8. Andy Smith was the only one of the recognised big names to have a decent grid position, on row 3, and took advantage to take the title. Paul Harrison took second, while John scrapped through for third; neither had a chance to fight for the lead since they were too concerned by their own battle for the podium. At the European Championship, John lost control and spun at a crucial moment. It put him out of the running and Rob Speak passed the chequered flag to take his first Formula 1 title.

It was a strong grid that lined up for the World Final, the third consecutive held at Coventry. Andy Smith won the second World Semi-Final and the coin toss to decide pole position; Frankie

Wainman Junior was on the outside of the front row. That put John on the inside of row 2 alongside Paul Harrison, while Ray Witts and Rob Speak made up row 4 behind two foreign entrants.

Smith predicted the fall of the green flag and leapt away from Wainman, who gave John enough space to follow Smith through the first turn into second. Wainman was right on John's back bumper and pushed him wide through the turn, but John kept Wainman behind. The pressure meant that John began to slide sideways on the far straight and threatened to spin, giving Wainman the chance to motor past. Paul Harrison's obliging bumper straightened John back up, but not before Ray Witts powered past and into the back end of Wainman's still-accelerating car. Wainman was left facing the wrong way on the turn at the end of the far straight, Witts was promoted to second while John was picking up speed again and moved into third. The rest of the field ploughed into or around Wainman, giving John time to recover. It took three laps for the pile-up to resolve itself, and yellow flags were shown on lap 4 to allow Wainman's car to be towed to the centre green.

On the restart the first four cars; Smith, Witts, John and Murray Harrison, were separated by two or three backmarkers who had escaped the pile-up. It gave each driver a cushion against immediate attack and allowed Smith to jet off and set the pace. John felt that his car was running well too, and he passed Witts by halfway through the race. Now about a quarter of a lap behind Smith, John clawed the gap back as Smith began to struggle to get power through his tyres and onto the track. When John went into a straight with American Josh Pelksy separating him from Smith, John went on the attack. Hitting Pelksy into Smith, John pushed both cars wide while retaining the inside line. He was into the lead and had only seven laps to survive.

John benefited from some good fortune. Smith had blown a head gasket, which was why John had been able to close the gap to a car which was previously the fastest in the race. It also meant that Smith was in no position to challenge for the lead again and he drove defensively for second, effectively acting as John's bodyguard. Smith kept his car going for second, while defending champion Murray Harrison got onto the podium with third.

Up to this point John had been racing with the shadow of Stuart Smith over him. In 1997 he equalled Smith's six World Championships, but the legendary driver still enjoyed a greater reputation. Now, for the first time, John eclipsed the Maestro. Seven World Final wins meant that John was the most successful World Champion in the history of stock car racing. Annette cried tears of joy, James and Sam joined in the victory celebrations and the twins joined their dad on the podium. John was happy and celebrated the World Final as much as any of his others, but not to any excess. The fact that he had now won more World Finals than anybody else meant little to him. He saw no value in comparing different drivers from different eras; he just wanted to win as many World Finals as he could.

John outlined his intent to focus on the major championships by building a new shale car at the start of the season and picking the meetings he attended. The decision paid off with the record-breaking World Final victory and third in the British Championship. It was not an unusual choice. Many drivers chose to concentrate on the major championships only as they reach the nadir of their racing career. Stuart Smith had done so in the mid-eighties and won three consecutive World Finals, more recently Dave Berresford had scaled back his racing activities in the early nineties but still aimed for the World Final each year in an attempt to secure the elusive gold roof. John stepped back from the slog of racing every weekend, sometimes three times in three days, to concentrate on the major championships.

However, the other inevitable result was that John also dropped back in the grading list and the National Points Championship. He won only one meeting final, at Sheffield on 31st October, his 199th meeting final win. He added seven other race wins, only one more than the disappointing 1999 campaign with the short wheelbase car. Frankie Wainman Junior took his fifth National Points Championship in a row and would eventually top the grading list for the next nine seasons, a record that surpassed even Stuart Smith. Having fallen as far back as seventh in the July grading list, John finished the season in fifth place, also behind Andy Smith, Paul Harrison and Mark Gilbank. Yet whereas the previous season seemed a failure, the performances at the World and British Championships made this one a success.

On each occasion that John won his first six World Championships, they came in twos: 1987 and 1988, 1991 and 1992, 1996 and 1997. He hoped to add 2000 and 2001 to that list and spent the winter preparing his cars for the new season as usual. Late in the off-season, however, John's preparations ground to an enforced halt.

On 19th February 2001, pigs at an abattoir in Essex tested positive for foot-and-mouth disease. Over the next few days and weeks, outbreaks of the disease spread to Cornwall, Devon, north Wales, south Scotland, Northumberland and the Lake District. At the end of March, just as the stock car season was due to start, the disease was at its height with up to fifty new cases a day. British pigs, sheep and cattle were banned from sale until the disease was eradicated; animals on infected farms were immediately culled and burned, many others on surrounding land were also killed. There was a complete halt on the movement of livestock and extensive measures were brought in to prevent humans spreading the disease from one site to another.

For a dairy farmer like John, the disease was potentially devastating. It got to within half a mile of his farm and John kept his cows isolated from external contact as much as possible. He initially took the cows to feed on land across the lane, but was told there was a risk of picking up the disease from the tarmac road. John had to lay a mat across the road, spread disinfectant on it, tramp the cows across, then carefully roll up the mat afterwards; repeating the process when the cows returned. It was so time-consuming that it was easier to keep the cows on one side of the road. All cars that visited the farm also had to be disinfected as soon as they turned off the tarmac.

At least Sam did well out of the crisis. The thirteen year old announced that it was far too dangerous for him to be travelling to school and back every day because surely he would transmit the disease on his shoes. He got to spend an enjoyable spring and summer on the farm helping out his father, and it confirmed his ambition to take over the family farm when he was old enough.

John had to pull out of a trip to race sprint cars in South Africa with Frankie Wainman Junior, Andy Smith, Derek Fairhurst and Danny Clarke; although since the meeting was a washout, John did not miss much. He made the effort to travel to two race meetings in May, at Coventry and Skegness, but needn't have bothered. The big block shale engine exploded at Coventry, leaving John with a major rebuilding job and difficulty sourcing parts. A week later he arrived at Skegness with his tarmac car to find out that they had rearranged the UK Open Championship to the previous day. Only in the Grand National at Skegness did things come good and John won a race. John started the last lap in third place, but a great last bend hit removed both Steve Cayzer and

Gary Castell. The sum total over the two meetings was one win, one third, one seventh, and three races that he did not finish.

The continuing crisis meant that stock car racing was forced to take a back seat. John was assured that the less comings and goings from the farm, the less chance there was of importing the disease. It was sensible not to risk it, especially considering that he would be driving his transporter bus into pits that were muddy, wet and filled with vehicles that had travelled around the country. He stayed away from stock car meetings for the next three months.

John was lucky. Foot-and-mouth did not spread to his farm. He slipped down the grading list and the gold roof was absent from nearly every meeting. John only retained his superstar status by virtue of the 'cannot be downgraded' rule, which allowed a successful driver to retain superstar or star grade for a fixed period.

John spent the enforced break lengthening the chassis on the short wheelbase tarmac car, making it 96 inches long like its shale sister, and cutting off the downtubes linking roll cage to bonnet to bumper. It was an admission that the short car had not performed as well as he hoped. Since the big block engine was still out of action, John put the small block engine in his shale car so he still had a ready-to-race car if an opportunity arose.

The incidence of new disease outbreaks slowed during the summer until John was confident enough to venture out in September. He was keen to put in an appearance at the World Championship meeting at Hednesford, one of his best tracks in the late eighties and early nineties, even if he would have to take up a spot at the back of the grid. He had that right as the reigning World Champion, and seized it since he had missed the World Semi-Finals (which he would not have qualified for anyway) and the Consolation Semi-Final.

John travelled to Hednesford on 2nd September, two weeks before the World Championship, to give his small block powered shale car a run out on the World Final track. After a steady start in which he qualified for the meeting final in seventh place, John then went out for another run in the consolation where he finished tenth. He lined up for the final with most spectators expecting little more than him giving his car another airing. Not a bit of it. John won the final, smacking Nick Smith midway round the last bend. Not only was he sending a signal that he would not allow his gold roof to be taken off him without a fight, it was also John's 200th meeting final win.

Of course, there was still little realistic chance of retaining the World Champion title. John lined up on the World Final grid a fortnight later in 34th place. He got off to a good start, roaring down the inside to gain thirteen places on the first lap as many cars slid into each other through the first corner. The pile-up gradually claimed more victims, including Frankie Wainman Junior, who was planted into the stranded cars by Andy Smith. The race was stopped after just three laps when it became obvious that Mark Woodhull was injured in the melee. A long stoppage during which Woodhull was cut from his car and taken to hospital by air ambulance added to the tension, and the race was eventually restarted under floodlights.

John did not get away as well on the second start. He clawed his way back through the field, passing one car after another, eventually working his way into sixth place. It was not enough. The chequered flag fell over Rob Speak; Wainman, Smith, Paul Harrison and Gary Castell remained in front of him.

John was philosophical. There was no point in getting upset about external events that he could not control. His sixth place was a good result, although it could have been even better had the first start not been ruled void. If he wanted to win the World

Championship again, he would simply have to come back next year and start all over again.

With the foot-and-mouth crisis now falling away, John raced in five meetings during the last grading period, making a total of nine for the season. He managed a meeting final win at Northampton and a second place at Sheffield. He also finished second in the Grand National Championship race at the Sheffield meeting, but most of the results were meaningless. John was just enjoying being out on track again. He was also already planning for next season.

Having missed so much of the previous season, John was eager to get going in 2002. Both cars were back in race worthy condition. The newly lengthened tarmac car was refitted with the small block engine; the restored big block engine was put back into the shale car. Now it was time to get them out on track again.

John made up for lost time by attending most race meetings in April and May. First place in the meeting finals at Coventry and Northampton, both World Championship qualifiers, were the high points of the first two months. At the UK Open Championship John finished one heat in fourth but did not qualify for the final. It was a similarly disappointing story at the Coventry-hosted British Championship, where John finished third in one heat and was not placed in his other. That earned a slot on the sixth row of the grid alongside Frankie Wainman Junior. Despite getting up to fourth place after four laps, John did not finish the race. Instead, a strong podium of Andy Smith, Rob Speak and Frankie Wainman Junior took the spoils.

After the last World Championship qualifier at Birmingham on 8th June, John stepped back from racing. Up to then he missed only some of the longer journeys like the annual meeting at the Arena Essex just off the M25. After the World Championship qualifiers were over, he picked the meetings that suited him and his championship prospects, much like he did in 2000. He raced three more times in June, three in July, four times in August and three in September.

Those meetings included the European Championship, held on the Northampton tarmac on 14th July. In the championship race, an early pile-up left Frankie Wainman Junior on the centre green. At half-distance defending champion Rob Speak cleared out Danny Clarke for the lead, though his hold on it was fragile since John and Paul Harrison were following closely. John shadowed him round the track, wary that he was in a vulnerable position in the middle of the three front runners. Just as he geared up for an attack, Speak drifted onto the centre green with a flat. That left John out in front with five laps to go and Harrison waiting behind. As the next two laps passed without an attack forthcoming, it became obvious that a last bend hit was inevitable. John waited, dropping his speed going into the first turn of the last lap, letting Harrison close up on the far straight. No longer having the room to build up speed, Harrison could only manage a tame tap on John's back bumper. John rode the hit well, sticking on the inside, bumping over the kerb, then accelerating hard out of the turn to win. Harrison limped across the line with two flat tyres courtesy of the kerb. Mark Gilbank, a driver who was hovering at the bottom of superstar grade, was third.

John registered another success in the World of Shale race at Belle Vue, beating Andy Smith and Gary Castell onto the lower steps of the podium. Frankie Wainman Junior had surged into an early lead with John second and Smith third. Finding himself in the middle of three strong runners, just like in the European Championship race, John decided to allow Smith past at half-distance. He then tracked Smith for the remaining laps, confident that he had the speed to take advantage of Smith's likely attack for first place. He had to wait until the last lap, at which point Smith drove Wainman into the fence but stalled. John went down the inside for first place, neither Smith nor Wainman able to do anything about it.

The path to the World Championship took John to Coventry, which would unusually host a World Semi-Final and World Final. The omens were good. The last time John won the World Final, in 2000, it was at Coventry. That year John started the World Semi-Final from third on the grid and pushed his way past one of the front rowers, Rob Speak, for second place behind Frankie Wainman Junior. This time, John started from third on the grid behind Wainman and Mark Gilbank. At the end of the race, John had knocked Gilbank into third and finished in second behind Wainman again. Perhaps history was going to repeat itself at Coventry in the big race.

Another parallel between the 2000 and 2002 World Championships was that Andy Smith won the second semi and shared the front row with Wainman again, just as he did two years before. This time Wainman won the coin toss, which put John on the outside of row 2. Rob Speak, the defending champion, sat on John's inside. Durk Greidanus and Louw Wobbes separated them from Mark Gilbank and Peter Falding on row 4. John's nerves were not helped when he took his grid position and his engine promptly stalled. It was reluctant to restart, but luckily the mechanics were still on the track and coaxed the big block Chevrolet back to life. A minute or two later the track was cleared and the rolling lap began.

Smith nosed into the lead down the home straight as the green flag fell and turned early on the first bend, forcing Wainman onto the infield. John and Speak slipped wide to get round the turn, but many of those behind did not find the same grip and crashed into the fence. Peter Falding was one of the few who had a good line and slipped by Speak, Wainman and John down the far straight. Waved yellow flags temporarily halted the race as the leaders rounded the first corner for a second time. Smith had managed to get in front of two backmarkers so had a cushion between himself and second placed Falding. John, Wainman and Speak were third, fourth and fifth.

The race settled down on the second restart and none of the top five drivers altered their position. Smith held the lead until the tenth lap, at which point he nudged his inside front wheel onto the kerb. Pressing down on the accelerator, the difference in traction between concrete and shale caused a half shaft to snap. With no power to one wheel, Smith could only guide his car onto the centre green. Falding looked to drift round Smith into the lead, but tangled with Louw Wobbes as he went through the corner and dropped out of the race. Instead it was John who whipped round the corner and into the lead. Wainman coasted to the centre green too a lap later too, another victim of a broken half shaft. Three of John's most dangerous opponents had dropped out within the space of two laps.

Now halfway through the race, John's only real challenger was Speak, who was still quite a distance back. Speak needed a helpful backmarker to throw a spanner in the works, but John drove cautiously, not leaving his back bumper exposed. Only at one point was he troubled, when two backmarkers tangled and blocked the track. John was forced to hug the outside fence to get past them and got through with inches to spare. After that, it was a case of counting down the laps to the chequered flag. By the time he passed it, every other driver except Speak and third placed Dave Johnson had been lapped.

It was the drive of a great champion. John was congratulated by many drivers on the track, and by both drivers and fans in the pits. One female Dutch fan was among those asking for the new

World Champion's autograph and John asked what she wanted signing. She lifted up her top and pointed to what she wanted. John duly signed her breast – anything for a fan – although he found it very difficult signing it while not looking at it. At least, that's what he told his wife!

John had now won eight World Championships, two more than Stuart Smith, and five more than the next nearest challengers, Johnny Brise and Dave Chisholm. Once again, his decision to step back from regular racing to concentrate on the biggest prize had paid off. He was truly the most successful stock car driver in the history of the sport.

All's good at Sheffield

14

The Next Generation
2003-2006

He may have been the most successful stock car driver in history, but John was not ready to finish yet. He began 2003 with a hunger as strong as ever. A podium place in each of his first three races at the Coventry opener was a good start to the season. Four meetings in, John registered his first race win in the meeting final at King's Lynn. A couple of weeks later came a second meeting final win, this time at Belle Vue. Not until 26th May did John fail to finish a meeting final. He was churning out consistent performances and keeping in touch with Frankie Wainman Junior at the top of the grading list.

The first two championships were a bit of a disappointment. The annual trip to Skegness for the UK Open Championship saw John finish in tenth. He was becoming fed up with the long trips to the east coast, and would not bother with the UK Open for the next couple of years. After 2003, he usually only appeared at Skegness when a World Championship qualifying round or semi-final demanded it. Northampton's European Championship, where John was the reigning champion, saw him lose the title to Paul Harrison. John finished in fifth, also behind Frankie Wainman Junior, Gary Castell and the Dutchman Bert Schaap Junior. However, John's eyes were fixed firmly on the World Championships.

He qualified for the World Semi-Final at Sheffield on the inside of the second row, with Frankie Wainman Junior and Paul Harrison in front. In a messy start, John found himself the middle of a stock car sandwich on the first turn. Wainman ending up facing sideways, pointing into the centre green, with John trapped behind, twisting sideways too, rammed by Neil Scothern. It was the opportunity that Harrison needed to break away and establish a clear lead that he held to the finish. Scothern mounted Wainman's bonnet in the collision and became stuck; John emerged unscathed, and once free of the melee got back to racing pace and finished in second. Murray Harrison worked his way up from row 8 for third; Wainman and Scothern had to make do with the back of the World Final grid after taking the first two places in the Consolation Semi-Final.

A couple of weeks after the first World Semi-Final, the best drivers arrived at Belle Vue for the British Championship. Frankie Wainman Junior had a perfect meeting, winning all three of his heats and the championship race, adding to his earlier success at the UK Open Championship. The other two places on the podium went to the next two drivers on the grid. Gary Castell finished second in each of his heats started second on the grid, while John got two seconds and a third and started on the inside of row

2. They swapped positions in the race; John worked his way one place up into second, while Castell finished third.

It was not a championship meeting that was remembered for close, exciting racing; instead it was marked by Wainman's clear dominance. However, two young drivers also made their mark for the first time. Each had a name and reputation to live up to. Stuart Smith Junior won a heat and came second in another. It was his first season of racing and he still had much to learn, but he showed promise. The second new driver was James Lund, driving a car numbered 153 in recognition of his father's famous 53. He was even earlier in his racing apprenticeship than Stuart Smith Junior and would finish races in only seven meetings in 2003. Nevertheless, he managed to finish each of his heats in the British Championship; in eighth, tenth and fifth.

Although his father was one of the most prolific stock car builders, James' first car was bought from Jason Holden. John helped out with a bit of advice, giving tips on how to set up the car correctly, but James was determined to stand on his own two feet. It was a slow learning curve, much more gradual than the one John had when he started racing, a consequence of changes in the sport over the past decades. No longer could a driver turn up and expect to be competitive in his first few meetings. Stock cars were now more finely tuned, driving styles and techniques had evolved over the years, race craft was more difficult to learn, and there were more regulations that had to be adhered to. Long gone were the days of a new driver spinning round the track causing chaos in his wake, like John did in 1976.

Second place in the British Championship was a decent boost to John's confidence, as was first place in the final at the last Coventry meeting before the World Championships. Since the World Final was also on the Coventry shale, John went there as the favourite to win again. Gary Castell and Paul Harrison led the way from the front row, with John on the inside of row 2 next to Mark Gilbank, and two foreign entrants behind. Still in with a chance were Peter Falding and Murray Harrison on row 4, while Lenny Smith and Stuart Smith Junior made up row 5. On the back row and seemingly out of it was Frankie Wainman Junior, while Andy Smith had failed to qualify at all.

It may have been a good opportunity for a ninth World Final win, but it was not to be. A heavily watered track meant that traction was hard to come by. Castell kept clear of Harrison as the cars slid along the home straight to start the race; John followed in third, then Gilbank. The slippery track caused Castell to spin on the on the second lap, while Gilbank clattered both John and Harrison in one manoeuvre. That allowed Peter Falding, Murray Harrison and Kiwi Neil McCoard through for the first three places.

The race was temporarily halted on lap 5, at which point John was sixth behind Falding, Murray Harrison, McCoard, Castell and Steve Cayzer, with Paul Harrison lurking in seventh. John pushed hard on the restart but drifted wide on the slick track and lost yet more time. By halfway through the race John was sat dejectedly on the centre green. Mechanical problems had forced him off the track, although he was never a serious contender anyway. Falding mastered the tricky conditions the best, winning his third World Championship.

In a decent run to the end of the season, John finished second in three consecutive meeting finals and third in another. He also won the last race in the finale meeting, the helter skelter at Hednesford. It all added up to fourth place in the National Points Championship, behind Wainman, Paul Harrison and Stuart Smith Junior.

*

A busy winter was ahead. Both Lunds wanted to take to the track in the new season with fresh cars. John sold his 2000 and 2002 World Final winning shale car to Roger Mitchell and took to the workshop to build a replacement. He was joined there by James. Having run his ex-Holden car for a year, he sold the chassis and kept the engine and gearbox for a self-built car of his own. Father and son started out side-by-side, each building a new car. John built a flat chassis as usual, ready to add the roll cage, axles and engine bay. James started out one step behind him, watching what John did and copying. But the younger Lund had more time on his hands and after a few weeks James was in the lead, taking advice from his father about what to do next.

The new cars were to take part in a milestone season. On 27th March 2004, the eve of the first meeting, invited guests gathered to celebrate stock car racing's golden jubilee. John was one of a handful of drivers still racing who also took part in the 25th year silver jubilee celebrations in 1979. One of the highlights of the evening was a presentation to ten individuals who had made a major contribution to the sport over the past fifty years. Drivers featured heavily. John's place on the list was almost guaranteed. He was joined by Stuart Smith, Willie Harrison, Frankie Wainman, Frankie Wainman Junior and Peter Falding. The other four awards went to promoter John La Trobe, fellow promoter and publisher of *Stock Car Magazine* Keith Barber, commentator Bev Greenhalf and starter Al Henderson.

The following day it was a young driver who took victory in the first meeting of the season at King's Lynn. Craig Finnikin, son of Bert, took the chequered flag to win his first meeting final. The second meeting of the season went back the way of the established old guard. John finished first in the meeting final at Coventry, the inaugural meeting in the Golden Jubilee Series, a competition marking the fiftieth season run in a similar format to the old Grand Prix Series. John did not approach the thirteen-round event with much commitment. He raced in only four meetings, leaving victory in the series to Frankie Wainman Junior.

John focused on the World Championship qualifying meetings instead. The number of these had nearly doubled from ten in 2003 to eighteen in 2004. John raced in fourteen, winning two and getting on the podium in three others. His commitment to meeting attendance in the qualifiers gave him pole position in the King's Lynn World Semi-Final. On paper it was also the easiest race, with Frankie Wainman Junior, Andy Smith and Peter Falding all at Buxton, but John failed to finish. Stuart Smith Junior took the win and Mark Gilbank was second. The time that John invested in the qualifying events rather than the Golden Jubilee Series came to nothing.

John had achieved little so far in 2004. He did not approach the Golden Jubilee Series with a serious bid for success, the World Championship had proved to be a failure, and he did not bother with the UK Open Championship at King's Lynn. On top of that, John trailed in a distant seventh at the European Championship on 18th July. Looking to recharge and refocus, John appeared in only one meeting in August and three in September.

At least there was some success for the Lund family. James got his new car on the grid for the first time at Buxton on 23rd May, and although he did not finish a race there, he had a great run of form in June. He won five races; Grand Nationals at Northampton and Knockhill, and heats at Cowdenbeath, Knockhill and King's Lynn. He leapfrogged up the grading list from white top to red top in one swoop. He did not pass the chequered flag first again for the rest of the season, but it proved that the Lund racing genes had been passed onto the next generation.

The World Final was hosted at Coventry, which established itself as the premier stock car venue by hosting its sixth World

Final in seven seasons. In a departure from normal procedure, the Consolation Semi-Final was ditched and a full race meeting held before the World Final. The first two drivers in the meeting final would then be given the final two grid slots for the World Final. John qualified for the meeting final with a smooth drive, finishing second in his heat, but his hopes of a World Final place were upended – literally – when he was dumped on his roof by a Dutch entrant. The crumpled aerofoil was now wrecked beyond recognition, although John was happy enough when a Dutch fan offered him a few pounds for the worthless, mangled metal.

Peter Falding came through from row 4 to win his fourth and final World Championship and become the third most successful driver at World Finals behind John and Stuart Smith. It propelled Falding into stock car history books, but he still did not achieve all that he might have done. It was Falding's misfortune that he reached his peak in the early nineties at the same time as John, otherwise he could easily have gone on to equal or pass Stuart Smith's tally of six World Championships himself, one of many drivers who could have won more titles were John not racing.

By late October, John was back on track, refreshed from his mid-season break and looking to take advantage of the two remaining chances for trophies. The first and best opportunity came at the British Championship, held back until the end of October due to the packed jubilee schedule. It was the first time Sheffield had hosted a major championship, and John hoped that the tight track with its lethal fence would benefit his skill and experience. Things were going well, and heat finishes of fourth, first and third gave John a good grid position, but he failed to finish in the championship race and Frankie Wainman Junior retained the title.

Only the Grand National Championship remained and Wainman took that too. John finished second, with Peter Falding third. The podium had the look of an early-nineties one, when John, Falding and Wainman were the three drivers dominating. But now each was looking over their shoulder at the new, upcoming generation of drivers like Stuart Smith Junior, Craig Finnikin and James Lund.

Although John's record of meeting final wins had dropped in recent years – he won three each in 2003, 2004 and 2005 – he always started the season well and got his first meeting win early in the season. The 2005 maiden win came at the second meeting, at Belle Vue. John followed the same pattern he had set over the last few seasons, racing regularly in April and May to build up World Championship qualifying points before stepping back after June to concentrate on the major championships.

This time, John struggled to pick up qualifying points and slipped back a couple of places in the rankings, starting the World Semi-Final at Skegness from the outside of row 2. Frankie Wainman Junior, Paul Harrison and Peter Falding were the three drivers who had finished above John in the rankings and started in front of him on the grid. John failed to finish, as did James who started on row 6. It meant that the World Championship would be out of reach for another year. Since the Consolation Semi-Final only offered a place on the back row of the World Final grid and would have meant a long journey to Wimbledon, John elected to stay away. The World Final, therefore, went the way of Frankie Wainman Junior, the second time that he had won the gold roof. Dave Schapp earned the best ever finish by a foreign driver in second, while Andy Smith was third.

That left two other major championships. The European Championship was won by Paul Hines, a young blue top who was beginning to force his way into star grade. John failed to finish. At the British Championship, hosted by Sheffield for the second year in a row, John started well. He finished his first two heats in second place, but slipped back to eighth in his last heat. That pushed him back to the outside of row 3, alongside Andy Smith. In front were Frankie Wainman Junior and Rob Cowley on row 2, and Stuart Smith Junior and Tom Harris at the front.

Andy Smith tried to get past Wainman on the first corner and pushed him from behind, but Smith's rear slipped out and John clattered into it. Both hit the fence and the rest of the pack ploughed into them. The track was jammed and a restart signalled, but both John and Smith had taken damage and were not on the grid for the restart. With two of the bigger names out of the running, it was left to a two-way struggle between Frankie Wainman Junior and Stuart Smith Junior. The race and title was eventually claimed by Wainman, which, when added to the World and National Points Championships, meant that he won the three biggest championships in one season: an achievement matched only by Ellis Ford in 1965, Stuart Smith in 1969 and John in 1987.

Although he had not taken part in much of the Golden Jubilee Series, John did decide to play a more comprehensive role in the 2005 Champions League, another competition based on the old Grand Prix Series format. He appeared at seven of the first eight rounds, although he did not finish in four of the meeting finals and dropped back out of contention. After the Birmingham round on 22nd October, which was the eighth consecutive meeting that he did not finish the final in the top ten, John called time on his season and skipped the last five meetings.

For John to go from mid-July to the end of the season without finishing a meeting final was almost unheard of. The last time he failed in eight consecutive finals was 1979. He needed to spend a bit of time in the workshop getting his cars back to optimum racing condition. It was not only his own car that needed work

on it, or that of James too. A third member was ready to join the
Lund Racing Team.

Sam was the keener of the two sons to get behind the wheel
and rarely missed a meeting when he started acting as mechanic
for his father. At the end of 2005, aged 17, Sam had taken part
in his first meeting at Birmingham using John's car, a new white
roof bearing the number 531 bolted on top. Although he had
been around farm machinery and tractors since a young age, and
although his father was a multiple World Champion, it was not
inevitable that Sam would be a successful driver. Nevertheless, he
seemed comfortable behind the wheel and drove his first meeting
like a natural, although he did not finish a race.

For the new season Sam, like James, started out with an ex-
Jason Holden car. Holden was selling his whole inventory having
decided to retire from racing, so Sam bought all his kit. This was
a considerable investment and John stepped in with a loan to
help him out with the cost. It looked to be money well spent.
Sam won the heat for white and yellow tops at the second meeting of the season; at the same meeting John won another heat.
Taking it slowly, just as James did in his first season, Sam finished
races at nine different meetings, including race wins at the World
Semi-Final and World Final meetings. While Sam was learning
the ropes, James decided to take a year out. He sold his two year
old car and went back to the workshop to build another. Taking
his time, James wanted to be ready to hit the ground running in
an attempt to secure and hold onto star grade.

At the first meeting of 2006 at King's Lynn, John finished
second in the meeting final and Grand National. John also gained
two other podium places in meeting finals in the busy period up
to the end of May, although none were in the valuable World
Championship qualifiers. That meant John had to start further

back in the World Semi-Final at King's Lynn, although it proved to be a blessing in disguise. Frankie Wainman Junior was sent into the fence on the first corner by Mark Gilbank, and the collision also trapped Peter Falding. John was able to slip by the chaos and take first place by the end of the race, ahead of Steve Cayzer and Lee Robinson.

The Coventry World Final was John's first since 2003 and his first on the front row since 1998. It was a great opportunity to win the gold roof again. The defending champion, Frankie Wainman Junior, started from the back having failed to finish in both the World Semi-Final and Consolation Semi-Final. Peter Falding had not made the grid at all, while Mark Gilbank had taken one of the consolation places towards the back and Paul Harrison languished on row 13. Stuart Smith Junior would also have to fight through the crowd from row 7. So it was his fellow front rower and pole sitter, Andy Smith, who was the biggest danger.

Smith edged ahead of John at the green flag, but John safely tucked in behind. Will Yarrow, who started behind John on the outside of the second row, was third. Initially the three ran close together; Smith was the first to edge clear, then John moved a safe distance in front of Yarrow. John needed to concentrate on closing up to the leader, who was flying through the backmarkers, but his hopes of keeping up were dashed when he tangled with a stray car. Although he was still in the race, John lost time and dropped behind Yarrow. John quickly retook second position, but Smith now seemed to be out of sight. It was a similar situation to Coventry in 2002. On that occasion, Smith held a secure lead from John but failed to take the chequered flag when mechanical failure intervened. John's only hope was that a similar slice of luck would take Smith out of the race.

But it was John upon whom the racing gods frowned on this occasion. As he nudged Dale Ewars from the racing line, the New

Zealander's car slipped sideways and John's outside front wheel clashed with Ewar's inside front. John slid onto the centre green before rejoining the race, but he was now slowed by a flat tyre. After running in second place for most of the race, John steadily slipped backwards to ninth. Andy Smith took the win, while a fantastic performance from Wainman saw him work his way past all but one of his 32 rivals for second place. Stuart Smith Junior was third.

Frankie Wainman Junior may have lost the gold roof, but he retained the British Championship at Ipswich. John had finished his two heats in eighth and tenth and had too much to do in the championship race, eventually coming home in sixth.

That left one title left for Wainman to defend, and the rules were changed to help his opponents take it. Wainman's dominance of the National Points Championship, having won ten in succession, led to a change in the way that the silver roof was awarded at the end of 2006. Points were usually accumulated over the whole season, a system which rewarded not only consistent drivers but those who could afford the costs incurred in travelling to all 57 race meetings. Instead, it was decided that the National Points Championship would be decided by the points accumulated in 35 designated race meetings.

If the new system was designed to encourage closer competition and greater interest in the points race, it worked. By the last meeting of the series, at Coventry on 4th November, the title had yet to be decided. Frankie Wainman Junior held a slender lead over Andy Smith, but it was whittled away as Smith won the Grand National Championship and meeting final. Although Wainman came second in the Grand National, Smith's fourth in the same race was enough to nudge past his rival to take the championship and force Wainman to race under an unfamiliar red roof the following year.

With the European Championship, at which John did not race, going to Wainman, it meant that all four major titles were shared between two drivers. It was the high point of the new Smith-Wainman rivalry, one which outshone even the original battles between Stuart Smith and Frankie Wainman in the late seventies and early eighties.

John had slipped back in the race to keep up with Wainman and Smith, although things were still looking good for the Lund Racing Team. Sam had got a difficult first season out of the way and was tipped as a potential star. James had his new car ready and hoped to push for a red top in the coming season. Some speculated that John would take a back seat in the coming season and allow his two boys to race more, but John was determined to stay out on track. He just wanted to win races, the World Championship in particular, and he was eager for another chance to wear the gold roof.

Three decades on and still a threat

15

Elder Statesman

2007 onwards

Saturday 13th January 2007 started much like any other winter day on the farm. The weather was poor; wet, windy and cold, but John was still up early to feed and sort out the cows.

By lunchtime Sam had arrived and was in the workshop, spending a few hours preparing his stock car for the new season. After that he turned to farm work, giving the cows their evening feed, while John got on with a few other tasks. As evening fell, Sam popped his head in the house to say goodbye before driving off to pick up his cousin and best friend, James Dewhurst. The two were inseparable and could be found in the local pubs and clubs most weekends. They had a typical Saturday night planned. Sam would usually pick up James from his house a mile down the road in Rimington then drive them both to his mother's house in

Gisburn. Sam could then get ready for the night out and the two of them would hit the town.

An hour or so after Sam left, the phone rang. It was Sarah, John's second wife and Sam's mother. Sam's friends had been ringing his mobile phone but got no response, so they had rung his home instead. Sarah wondered whether Sam had fallen asleep on the sofa. It was still blowing a gale outside and John was immediately worried. He set off in his car towards Gisburn, tracing Sam's route.

A couple of miles down the road, John saw flashing blue lights. His stomach churned. A policeman stopped John's car and said that there had been an accident. John asked if it was a Peugeot 205. It was. John told the policeman that he thought he was the father of the driver.

John could tell by the tone of the policeman's voice that something was seriously wrong. He asked to get past, but was told that the driver had already been taken away in an ambulance. The policeman would not let John drive to the hospital himself, so an officer got in the driver's seat and drove him there. John overheard a message relayed over the police radio saying that the passenger in the car – his nephew, James – was dead.

Sam was unconscious. For five days, John and Sarah maintained a vigil at his bedside at the Royal Blackburn Hospital. The doctors did all they could, but Sam succumbed to massive head injuries on Thursday 18th January. Sam was nineteen years old, James was sixteen.

It was the worst moment of John's life.

In a small community where everybody knows each other, a double fatality was a genuine tragedy that rocked the whole neighbourhood. The funeral cortege passed by the schools that Sam and James attended; both teachers and pupils lined up on the side of the road as the hearse went past. Hundreds of mourners packed Gisburn Parish Church for the joint funeral, while more than 200 other well-wishers listened to the service in the church-yard by loudspeaker and heard the two bereaved fathers read out a moving tribute. Sam's stock car was parked up outside the church, a poignant reminder that a promising motorsport career had been cut short.

John's poor start to the 2007 stock car season was entirely ex-cusable. He did not finish in the top ten in the finals of each of his first five meetings, three of which were World Champion-ship qualifying meetings. Once John started to grind out finishes again he managed sixth in the qualifying meeting at Sheffield and fourth at Belle Vue, but did not appear at the Wimbledon, Skeg-ness, Buxton, King's Lynn and Cowdenbeath rounds.

For the first time, World Championship qualifying rounds had also been run at the end of the previous season in an attempt to create excitement and interest in the post-World Final meet-ings. Unfortunately for John he had fared little better in those. He finished eighth in the meeting final at Northampton, but did not attend Sheffield and King's Lynn.

It was a dark time, and John realised that life would never be the same again, but by midsummer the worst of his grief was be-ginning to subside. Stock car racing gave him something to focus on, something to take his mind off the cruel events of the winter. He got back into the workshop and spent some time bringing his car back to racing pace. First place in the consolation at Coventry on 7th July was followed up with a win in the meeting final. Two weeks later it was time for John's World Semi-Final. He was al-located a place in the Sheffield race and started on row 5. There were eight cars in front of him when the green flag was waved, but by the chequered flag John had worked his way up to fourth.

Andy Smith, Matt Newson and Peter Falding made up the podium.

John's form was picking up. He finished second in a meeting final at Coventry on 2nd August and won the meeting final at Belle Vue on 26th August. It was all good preparation for the World Championship at King's Lynn, a stadium which had been upgraded and modernised for the flagship event. John started on row 5 alongside Derek Fairhurst. In front of him was a strong group of drivers who were each capable of winning the race. Peter Falding was looking for his fifth title, Frankie Wainman Junior and Andy Smith each wanted their third. Mark Gilbank was an experienced star grade driver, while Stuart Smith Junior was a youngster with obvious potential. Matt Newson, another relative newcomer, was a Norfolk-based driver with excellent local knowledge of the King's Lynn shale. Dave Schapp, one of the two foreigners on row 3, had gone as close as second place in 2005.

The start was probably John's worst in a World Final. John was wedged up against the fence by Fairhurst as the cars accelerated round the turn before passing the green flag on the home straight. His wheel dug against the fence and the car shuddered to a halt while the rest of the field flooded past him. Once the final car was past, John reversed out and got going again. Andy Smith was already bearing down on him and John looked like he was going to be the first car to be lapped, barely metres past the start line. He just kept clear of Smith, then caught up to the rear of the chasing pack on the second lap when waved yellow flags slowed everybody down. Although John was back in the race, his car had obvious front end damage and he managed only one more lap before calling it a day. The gold roof ended up switching cars, but it stayed in the Smith family. Stuart Smith Junior won the race, ahead of Frankie Wainman Junior and Andy Smith.

John did not bother with the British Championship at Skegness in October. He was sharing race meetings and the workload on the farm with James, and often only one of the two Lund drivers appeared on track at a race meeting. James struggled at the British Championship, with only one eighth place to show from his three heats, but did much better elsewhere. He won heat, final and Grand National at Birmingham on 25th August, and nearly did the same at the next meeting on that track on 8th September, finishing first in heat and Grand National but second in the meeting final. He also finished sixth in the Grand National Championship race (which John did not finish), and followed that with victory in the meeting final.

John had already given up on 2007. The year could not finish quick enough for him. He eyed up the World Championship in 2008, the number of qualifying meetings for which had increased again and now numbered sixteen rounds. Three of them were at the end of 2007, and John finished third in the meeting final at Sheffield to earn his first qualifying points for the next season.

Car 53 now housed the undisputed elder statesman of racing. Frankie Wainman retired at the end of the 2007 season; Peter Falding (who actually started seven years after John) would go at the end of the next. No current driver came close to John's unbroken career in the sport. John still sat comfortably under a red roof in star grade, proof that he was still a contender for the major championships.

There were, of course, some changes now that John was in his twilight years. A new year dawned, but the same Lund cars appeared on track. John no longer had time to build a new one each winter; farm work kept him too busy. John also did not change his pattern of racing from the previous year. He did not bother with most long distance trips to Skegness, King's Lynn, Bristol,

Cowdenbeath and Knockhill; and left Birmingham and Buxton to James, whose best results were on tarmac. That left John with meeting final finishes in four of the World Championship rounds, each on shale: twice at Sheffield, also Coventry and Belle Vue.

Like it or not, John would have a long drive for his World Semi-Final. One was hosted by Skegness, the other King's Lynn. Both John and James were allocated King's Lynn, John from the inside of row 3, and James the outside of row 13. World Semi-Finals were often pedestrian affairs, with drivers simply happy to progress to the World Final. This race was more intense. Frankie Wainman Junior kept the lead from pole, but Andy Smith and Mark Gilbank traded second place three times in the first couple of laps. John's car was initially slow and he was pressured by Michael Scriven, Tom Harris and Chris Fort. John held them off for a lap or two but then dropped back to seventh as they forced their way past. He tried to immediately retake the lost places by knocking Scriven into Fort, putting both wide. He succeeded in getting inside Scriven, but Fort held his speed and place. A lap later John was on the receiving end as Mick Harris hit him hard against the fence. John survived, but Scriven and Carlos Perez got past. Harris suffered damage and was forced to quit.

A pile-up put James out of the race and brought out waved yellow flags, allowing John to draw breath. He was now in eighth. He gained a place shortly after the restart when Fort was despatched into the fence, and remained in seventh until there were five laps left to run. John was temporarily out of the melee, but those in front were constantly trading places with plenty of bumper work. That meant another temporary halt was almost inevitable, after which John nudged Scriven wide for sixth place. Tom Harris and Gilbank were both late casualties of passing manoeuvres, promoting John further. By the time he passed the chequered flag John qualified in fourth place, behind Andy Smith, Frankie Wainman

Junior and Carlos Perez. It was a gruelling and tough race, but a good result.

For the second season in a row, John started the World Final on the outside of row 5. It also necessitated another long drive, this time to Ipswich. The tarmac surface there did not suit John's current setup, but he tried to find some speed on the hard stuff with some long distance trips to Ipswich, Hednesford, Buxton, Northampton and Skegness (twice) in the three months leading to the World Championship meeting.

Once again, it was a strong grid. Andy Smith and Paul Harrison made up the front row, with Stuart Smith Junior and Frankie Wainman Junior behind. The two foreigners on row 3, Louw Wobbes and Ron Kroonder, hoped to break the long-held British dominance of the World Final. On rows 4 and 5 were Carlos Perez, Matt Newson, Paul Hines and John; each hoped to take advantage of any mistakes by the front six.

Unfortunately for them, the front rowers got through the first couple of laps without mishap and the race settled down. John circled the track for the first half of the race consistently, maintaining position and taking advantage when any of the front runners dropped out. Although he was far from the battle for the lead, he could easily scrape onto the podium if those in front had any problems. Those hopes were dashed at half-distance when Dave Berresford's engine exploded, spreading oil on the track. John was one of three drivers following fairly closely who had little time to react. He slipped on the oil and clattered the fence, tangling with Murray Harrison and Hines. John managed to keep going, but his hopes of a podium finish were now gone and he finished the race in twelfth. Andy Smith held the lead from Harrison until the chequered flag, while Kroonder made it onto the podium in third.

The British Championship was held at Coventry, a more conveniently-sited track with a shale surface. John finished tenth and seventh in his two heats, not a great performance, meaning that he started on the inside of row 11 in the championship race.

To make progress John needed a few cars to dump themselves out on the first turn and a few race stoppages to catch up any distance lost. He got both. The opening lap saw cars spinning off all round the track and John picked his way through the mayhem into seventh. The yellow flags inevitably came out on lap 2, which bunched up the field and helped John catch up to the front runners. The leaders continued to drop like flies, promoting John to fourth. Again, the yellows came out and John caught up to the drivers in front of him; now only Mark Gilbank, Stuart Smith Junior and Frankie Wainman Junior stood between him and victory. John then took advantage of Wainman's hit on Smith to take third place, but Stuart's older brother Andy quickly nabbed the place from John, followed by Tom Harris, then Stuart recovered to pass too.

John was now back in sixth and struggling to match the pace of the quickest cars, but continued to progress when Andy Smith and Gilbank were sent into the fence. John's only overtaking manoeuvre was to pass Harris, and although it was slightly botched and the two cars clambered on each other, John came out of it in third place. Stuart Smith Junior was clear of Frankie Wainman Junior, who in turn had a good lead over John. The positions stayed that way until the end. John claimed his first major championship podium since 2003.

For the first time in a few years, John raced right through to the final meeting of the season, the gala night event at Birmingham. It was a good decision. He won his third meeting final of the season, holding off Frankie Wainman Junior and Paul Harrison to the chequered flag, finishing the season on a high.

*

John's racing record after 2003 was similar to the kind of form that he had in the early-eighties. He usually qualified for the meeting final and mostly finished those in the top ten with an occasional meeting final victory and an occasional failure. He was safe in star grade, never under threat of dropping back to a blue top. Although he was not the favourite to win races and major championships, he could not be discounted because a good drive and a bit of luck could see him pass the chequered flag first.

The difference between the early-eighties and the current situation, however, was the pressure of history. He was the most successful World Champion in the history of the sport, and high expectations weighed heavily on John's shoulders. How he dealt with it was crucial to the later years of his career.

Some men might crack under the pressure, become frustrated that they were no longer in the fastest car on track, and retire from the sport. That was not how John approached racing. He stuck by the same, reliable approach he always had: he just went out to win races. If it didn't happen, then he went out to win the next race instead. And the next one. And the next one.

The pressure was actually on his opponents. Drivers out on track would see number 53 just behind or in front and realised that this was not just another red top, but a racing legend. How would they deal with John Lund? Some would let him by; others would react over-aggressively, but that would increase their chances of making a mistake. The best way to deal with John was to treat him like just another driver – but that was difficult to do knowing his many achievements.

While James continued to focus on tarmac, winning a heat and final at Birmingham, John sought out success on both surfaces. He returned to Northampton for the European Championship in July, where Lee Fairhurst and Stuart Smith Junior broke away from the rest of the field for first and second. John was in with a chance of the podium but the chasing pack was large, comprising John, Spencer Taylor, Mark Gilbank, Dan Johnson and Paul Hines. The scrap eventually resolved with Gilbank in third, John had to settle for seventh.

John did not finish in the top ten in the meeting final of each of the vital World Championship qualifiers he attended from the first round in October 2008 to the end of May 2009. Knowing that he was falling behind in the chase for a good grid slot, John took the unusual step of travelling up to Scotland for the meetings at Knockhill and Cowdenbeath, where he finally broke his duck with finishes of tenth and eighth. Together with ninth at King's Lynn, John had done enough for a reasonable position on the outside of row 4 at Coventry.

John made up a few places on the first turn as Lee Fairhurst connected with the fence, but promptly lost it – and more – when Murray Harrison shoved him into Mark Gilbank on the next turn. John got back on track and was running four cars behind the leader, but he had already been lapped and was actually last. He now had to claw his way back through the field, but any chance of a decent position in the World Final had gone. John came agonisingly close to qualification, finishing the race in eleventh, one spot shy of a World Final berth. Instead he had to go to King's Lynn for the Consolation Semi-Final. As the only recognised top driver on the grid, he was the favourite to win. He did so; Simon Panton claimed the other World Final berth.

Starting at the back of the World Final grid, John might have been a good outside bet for the title in past years. When he took up a similar position in 1994 and 2001 he came through the field for sixth, while in 1989 he finished tenth. By 2009, however, John was a less formidable threat. Andy Smith drove from the front row to retain his title, while John's only moment of note came when he was lapped by the leader. The lesson was clear. If John wanted to beat the Smith brothers and Frankie Wainman Junior, he would have to ensure a good grid position.

The lesson was reinforced almost immediately. At the British Championship at Belle Vue, three weeks later, John finished two heats in fifth and fourth but failed in the third. That put him in the middle of the pack on the inside of row 8. It gave John an outside chance, but he was never close enough to challenge for the lead. Stuart Smith Junior and Andy Smith made up the front row, with their ever-present rival, Frankie Wainman Junior, on the inside of row 2. Both Smiths slipped down the field after brushes with the fence, while Wainman was shunted into the fence on the second lap.

Their misfortune benefited the drivers behind, and John worked his way into third place behind Lee Robinson and Tom Harris. Yet as John gained on Harris, Andy Smith was rediscovering his speed and was gaining on John. Going into a corner, John went on the attack. He hit Harris and although he did not get past, Harris was forced to turn onto the centre green with mechanical problems. John's stay in second place was short lived. Smith attacked on the following lap, knocking John wide. Although John nibbled back on the next corner, he was not able to retake second. Any thoughts of carrying on the attacks disappeared when John saw Mark Gilbank gaining on him. John spent the second half of the race driving defensively, holding off Gilbank while Smith went on to pass Robinson.

It was the second year in a row that John had achieved third place in the British Championship. His success reflected the nature of the meeting, which played to John's strengths. With each driver racing in three heats and getting a chance to watch another five from the sidelines, it provided an excellent opportunity for drivers to slightly alter their car setup in response to the conditions on the track. The ability to recognise how conditions were changing and how a car could be changed to take advantage is something that can only be gained by experience. And experience was something that John had in bucket loads.

On the other hand, major races like the World Semi-Final or World Final tended to be run at the start of a race meeting and required a car to be running in optimum condition right from the start. The more often a driver raced, the more likely he was to have his car perfect from the start. John, aware that he was coming towards the end of his career and with a busy farm to supervise, could no longer spend the time and money racing at every meeting, nor could he arrive early at tracks and attend pre-meeting practice sessions.

The National Points Championship was tinkered with again in an attempt to keep spectators coming through the turnstiles for the last two or three months of the season. This time, the top ten scoring drivers after 25 allocated meetings had their points zeroed and raced again in a ten meeting National Series Shootout. John was not among them. He finished outside the qualifying positions in twelfth place on 219 points, some way from Lee Robinson's 290 in tenth. Although he won two meetings finals during the season, both at Coventry, they came after the cut-off point to decide the ten drivers in the shootout.

The first Coventry win was even more extraordinary since John was effectively driving with one eye, the result of a freakish farming accident. While balanced on a gate to pour some treacle into a feed box for the cows, John felt the gate begin to swing. He toppled over, catching his foot in the fence, and took the impact of the floor just above his right eye. His face was a mess, he needed stitches to stem the bleeding from his cut forehead and his right eye closed up like a boxer who has taken a blow. But John didn't bother about a bit of pain, he was used to it.

Farming was the kind of job that required manual labour, and occasional accidents were a fact of life. John raced in the 2004 World Championship meeting (the one in which he rolled in the meeting final) with a damaged shoulder, having slipped between two sacks of sawdust while carrying a tray of tea – although he didn't spill a drop! He also had a spring slice through his lip when his father let a gate go and it ricocheted into John. But John's most spectacular 'You've Been Framed' moment was when a bull tossed him across a fence. He was lucky that he landed on the safe side of the fence, otherwise the bull might have continued the attack. But he was unlucky that he turned in the air and the barbed wire caught the back of his jeans. John landed on his head, suddenly without trousers, leaving his jeans dangling on the wire!

John was still dedicated to the quest for a ninth World Championship. He turned out for his first meeting of 2010 sporting a redesigned bumper and sidebars, hoping to strengthen his chassis and protect his fragile wheels and tyres from the fences. Using this new setup he attended eleven out of fourteen World Championship qualifiers, although meeting final finishes frustratingly avoided him on six occasions. Nevertheless, a win in the meeting final at King's Lynn did enough to promote John to the inside of row 3 at the Buxton World Semi-Final. The inside of the first three rows went on to take the first three places; Andy Smith won, Paul Hines was second and John third. Those on the outside; Tom Harris, Mark Gilbank and Scott Davids, gradually dropped away and out of the race and would have to try their chances in the Consolation Semi-Final.

James did not qualify for the World Final, having started the same World Semi-Final from row 7, but put that disappointment aside to win the meeting consolation and final. He also performed commendably at the other major championships. At the European Championship he just missed out on the podium in fourth place, bumpered out of the way on the last bend by Chris Cowley. John was ninth. James also outperformed his father at the British Championship. He won a heat and was the tenth-highest ranked driver after the heats, a position in which he remained at the end of the championship race. John failed to finish either of his heats, getting spun out by Dan Johnson in his first and knocked out of the way by James in his second.

The World Final remained John's priority. His struggle from the back of the grid in 2009 made John realise that he would need a decent grid position if he were to win the World Final again. This time he had it. Frankie Wainman Junior lined up at Coventry on pole, with defending champion Andy Smith next to him. Paul Hines and Paul Harrison sat on row 2, with Ron Kroonder and Louw Wobbes on row 3. John had the outside of row 4 with Dan Johnson on his inside. As the cars were introduced, Wainman and Smith supporters each cheered their favourite. The biggest cheer, however, went to John. He was humbled by the support that the majority of the crowd showed towards him. Although Wainman and Smith had their loyal fan bases, John was everybody's second-favourite driver.

Smith was in the best position to take victory, but he had to get clear of the drivers who wanted to stop him winning a third consecutive World Championship. Realising that he was exposed, Smith raced down the home straight as the green flag fell. The pack of cars behind fought to keep up with him and clattered into each other on the first turn. Johnson rolled; Harrison, Kroonder and Wobbes went into the fence, John and Matt Newson were pulled into the pile-up. Smith and Wainman tore away, but few others followed them as the track was blocked. The officials had no option but to call for a restart.

In the long delay between the first and second starts, John pulled onto the centre green and viewed the damage to his car. It was clear that he was going to struggle to make the restart. He started work immediately, fighting to get his wheel off and a spare on. Surrounded by other drivers who were helping out, including non-qualifier Rob Cowley who sprinted from the pits to the track with a spare wheel, John worked feverishly. Some thirty minutes later, as the cars were forming the grid again, John fired up his car and returned to the track. The cheers of the crowd were almost as loud as if he had won the race.

At the restart, John's grid position improved considerably. The two cars in front of him, Wobbes and Harrison, were unable to make the second start. Although he was on row 4, there was now a clear space between John and front-rower Smith. It meant that John had room to manoeuvre as the green flag fell and he made up a couple of places, but then he got hooked up on another car on the far straight and connected with the fence, losing ground on the leaders. When he got back going, his steering was not functioning properly. The damage that John had taken in his collisions with the fence began to tell and John pulled onto the centre green for the second time, this time out of the race for good.

Smith went on to win the race, his third consecutive World Championship title, achieving one of the few honours that John had not. Smith also moved clear of Peter Falding in the history books with five World Championships. For the sixth time, Wainman had to settle for second.

Even though he failed to make an impact in the race, the reaction to John's appearance on track and the roar of the crowd as his car returned for the restart indicated that John had won another achievement: surely he was now one of the most popular drivers of all time. Spectators and drivers alike wanted him to hang on as long as possible, eager to watch a stock car legend while he still competed, hoping for one last big success.

They recognised one of the greatest careers in motorsport. Nobody else is an eight-time World Champion. Also six-time National Points Champion. Six-time British Champion. Three-time European Champion. Long Track World Champion. Eight-time Grand National Champion. Three-time UK Open Champion. Scottish Champion. Five-time Grand Prix Series winner. Over 220 meeting final victories. Over 800 race wins.

The only other drivers who come close to John's long list of achievements are Stuart Smith and Frankie Wainman Junior. Andy Smith still has a chance to expand the triumvirate of the most successful drivers, but has some way to go yet.

John achieved his success with a combination of driving skill, technical innovation, determination and bravery. Sure, there was a little luck too, but in a career spanning nearly four decades luck tends to even itself out, and there were occasions in which John was unlucky not to add to his vast trophy collection too.

John has beaten some excellent drivers into second place over the years. Peter Falding was his main rival from the mid-eighties to the mid-nineties, replaced by Frankie Wainman Junior for the next ten years. There were many others too: Dave Berresford, Bobby Burns, Bert Finnikin, Paul Harrison, Ron Kroonder, Andy Smith, Ray Tyldesley, Frankie Wainman and Nigel Whorton. Each would probably have had more success in their careers had they not the misfortune of racing at the same time as John.

But perhaps the most remarkable thing is that all this success has gone to a quiet, unassuming man. There is no hint of arrogance or self-confidence in his manner. He is grounded, a salt-of-the-earth Lancastrian, committed to his family and his business. And, if time allows, he just loves going out on track, always looking to win every race in which he competes.

Especially if that race is the World Final.

Afterword

By John Lund

It has been a pleasure and a privilege to be involved in stock cars for what seems like a very long time! I'm grateful that I've been part of this unbelievable sport. Although stock car racing might not always look the friendliest of sports, with bumpers being stuck in all round the track, I consider all the other drivers to be friends and I like to think that they would say the same about me.

Living and working in the same place means that it is easy to get isolated. I don't see many people on the farm, and I would get stuck in my own little bubble if I couldn't go to race meetings or friends didn't come to work on the stock car in the evenings. Stock car racing gives me a broader viewpoint on life. It's a release from my day job. I always look forward to taking my wellies off and putting my racing boots on!

So I count myself lucky. I like to think I'd have raced for as long as I have even if I hadn't had any success. Winning races and winning championships is nice, but to use a well-worn phrase, it's the taking part that counts!

But I wouldn't have been able to race at all if it wasn't for the many people who have helped me over the years. Naming them all individually would take a book in itself, and I'd be sure to forget somebody. So instead I'd like to thank you all together.

Stock car racing, although cheap compared with many formulas, still takes a bit of money. A number of different sponsors have helped me out in that regard. For all those who opened their wallets a little for me, thank you.

Many different people have helped me get the car on track. Preparing a stock car takes time, with long hours in the workshop in the evening and in the pits on race day. So thank you to all who have got their hands dirty on my behalf.

Others were never seen at the race track because they stayed behind to look after the farm while I went to race. I've had some great lads work on the farm over the years, and I really value their help.

My family are the most important thing to me. If they said I couldn't race, then I wouldn't, although I might get a little bit grumpy! But I appreciate the help that all my family have given me over the years, especially Annette, James, Abbie and Amy; and also Sam, who will never be forgotten.

Finally, thank you to the fans. I have spoken to many people in the pits over the years. Some I know by name, others I just know their faces. And there are many more who have cheered me on from the terraces. It definitely helps to motivate me. But the biggest help that the fans ever gave me was after Sam died. I was overwhelmed by the cards and letters I received, from people I never knew but who took the time to think of me. They helped to get me through a difficult time. Thank you all very much. I hope that you've got a little bit of pleasure watching me race, because I've certainly enjoyed being behind the steering wheel!

Career Achievements

World Champion: 1987, 1988, 1991, 1992, 1996, 1997, 2000, 2002

National Points Champion: 1987, 1988, 1989, 1990, 1991, 1992
British Champion: 1987, 1989, 1990, 1995, 1997, 1998
European Champion: 1989, 1992, 2002

Long Track World Champion: 1990
BriSCA Supreme Champion: 1989
Grand National Champion: 1986, 1987, 1988, 1989, 1990, 1991, 1994, 1998
Grand Prix Series Winner: 1987, 1988, 1990, 1993, 1997
Scottish Champion: 1986
UK Open Champion: 1990, 1992, 1994

Race Wins By Track:		Race Wins By Year:	
Aycliffe	75	1976	5
Belle Vue (76-87)	15	1977	10
Belle Vue (99-)	11	1978	8
Birmingham	5	1979	10
Blackburn	21	1980	10
Bolton	2	1981	30
Boston	22	1982	32
Bradford	88	1983	34
Buxton	19	1984	19
Cleethorpes	1	1985	9
Coventry	75	1986	54
Crewe	46	1987	53
Hartlepool	42	1988	101
Hednesford	33	1989	80
King's Lynn	28	1990	60
Leicester	2	1991	47
Long Eaton	49	1992	46
Mildenhall	4	1993	21
Nelson	7	1994	26
Newcastle	2	1995	28
Newtongrange	4	1996	21
Northampton	78	1997	21
Rochdale	35	1998	14
Scunthorpe	26	1999	7
Sheffield	42	2000	8
Skegness	43	2001	5
Stoke	20	2002	6
Swaffham	1	2003	5
Swindon	1	2004	6
White City	8	2005	5
Wimbledon	1	2006	6
		2007	7
Total	806	2008	4
		2009	7
		2010	1
		Total	806

Index

Buy copies of the images in this book from

Mike Greenwood's Photostox
www.photostox.com

Chequered Flag
PUBLISHING

www.chequeredflagpublishing.co.uk